Get Over Yourself,

DECIDE TO LEAD

Insights from Hard Lessons Learned

Get Over Yourself,

DECIDE TO LEAD

Insights from Hard Lessons Learned

WAYNE STRICKLAND
WITH TINA WENDLING

Get Over Yourself, Decide to Lead: Insights from Hard Lessons Learned by Wayne Strickland with Tina Wendling

Cover design by Overflow Story Lab

Interior design by Margaret Haik

ISBN-13: 978-1985581722
ISBN-10: 1985581728

CreateSpace Independent Publishing Platform
North Charleston, South Carolina
Printed in the United States of America

Available at Amazon.com and other book retailers.

For my father, JC Strickland

Contents

Acknowledgements i
Introduction: Why I Wrote this Book v

Part One: Build from the Ground Up 1
Chapter 1 Why have a philosophy? 2
Chapter 2 An Early Gift 9
Chapter 3 The Most Important Lesson 17

Part Two: My Leadership Philosophy 21
COMMUNICATION 23
Chapter 4 Get to Know Your Team and Let Them Get to Know You... 24
Chapter 5 Explain Your Nits 32
Chapter 6 Define Expectations 43
Chapter 7 Determine and Articulate your Work Style 51
Chapter 8 Listen Carefully and Ask Good Questions 59
Chapter 9 Double-Edged Sword 67

COURAGE 72
Chapter 10 Cultivate Courage over Time 74
Chapter 11 Make Decisions and Manage Tension 78
Chapter 12 Hold Yourself Accountable and Give Your Team Credit 82
Chapter 13 Keep Your Mouth Shut 86
Chapter 14 Achieve Balance 90

CLARITY 102
Chapter 15 Build Your Brand 104
Chapter 16 Be Aware of Your Own Optics 110
Chapter 17 What Gets Measured Gets Done 114
Chapter 18 Stop the Drama 118

CONVICTION 123
Chapter 19 Understand the Marketplace 124
Chapter 20 The Best Team Wins 129
Chapter 21 Lead from Top to Bottom 137
Chapter 22 Lead into the Future 143

Part Three: The Education of Experience 153
Chapter 23 Learning to Close the Deal 154
Chapter 24 On the Job Training 158
Chapter 25 Under the Gun 168
Chapter 26 Enjoy the Journey and Don't Take Yourself Too Seriously 179
Chapter 27 At the End of the Day 187

Suggested Further Reading 192
About the Authors 195

Acknowledgements

MY FAMILY IS MY inspiration. I want to thank them for the joy and texture they bring to my life. They are the reason for everything.

First, I want to thank my wife, Aviva, for driving me to complete this book while working full-time in corporate life. I am certain that neither edition of this book would exist today without her full support. Thank you, Aviva.

I want to recognize our children. Our daughter McCall, her husband, Jamie, and our sweet grandchildren Reese and Jake live in Kansas City. McCall is a great mom who volunteers at the KC Pet Project several times a week. Jamie took a big risk a few years ago to start his own business and has developed a thriving, profitable business and has a very bright future.

Our son, Joshua, his wife, Megan, and our adorable grandson Graham live in Melbourne, Australia. Joshua is the Australia brand manager for Felt Bikes, the maker of cutting-edge, world-class bikes, and has completed ten International Ironman Races. He is highly ranked in the US and in the world in his age bracket. Megan is in her seventh year with Cerner, has had multiple promotions, and currently leads a major division of the Cerner business in Australia.

Our daughter Caroline and her husband, Jon, a doctor of physical therapy with Mosaic, live in Kansas City. She also works for Cerner, currently managing her first team in a fast-growing company. We expect her to continue to excel in her career.

Our youngest daughter Asha is in eleventh grade at The Pembroke Hill School in Kansas City. We believe she is on her way to making an impact creatively in the world. She is truly our creative talent.

I have been blessed to work for a great company with a superior brand, run by a family that cares about the community, its employees, its customers, and the consumers who buy its products for over thirty-eight years. I have been given a rare gift to grow up in the company and work many times with the two grandsons of the founder. Don and Dave Hall, currently the CEO and president, have inspired my personal and professional growth with the choices they make every day both in and outside of work. They have always taken the long view versus what others might see as urgent or critical today, and they have always done what's right for the people they care most about, their employees, customers, consumers, and the Kansas City community. Both are incredible men that walk the walk with their employees and their families.

After finishing a book that is a summary of almost forty years of lessons learned, I wish I could recognize all the people who have influenced my career, but it's likely I can't remember them all. Here are a few that have clearly made a difference:

Lanny Julian, the best chief customer officer I have ever seen. Homer Evans, my original mentor, who exemplified the best of professionalism and thoroughness. He did everything with class and dignity. Tim Scheele, one of the smartest people I have ever worked for. Doranne Hudson, a terrific leader from whom I learned a tremendous amount at a critical time in my career. Jim Welch, a true growth leader who can do just about anything. John Dye, an incredible leader, a world class consultant, friend, and coach. Dean Erlandson, a great leader, a great man, and a great friend. Patrick Gahagan, long-term friend who has achieved just the right balance between his professional life, his personal life, and his faith. Rick Riddle, another long-term friend who is always there when you need him. Ellen Karp, "Coach K," responsible for sparking my career turn around. Jeff Brinkman, pastor, friend, handy-man, and all around good guy. Mike Perry, the current president of Hallmark Greetings, who encourages big thinking and big risk-taking and creates a culture perfect for both.

I am sure there are many more, and to each and every one, I say a heartfelt THANK YOU.

Introduction

Why I Wrote This Book

We were almost ready to get out of there when I heard the distinctive sound of a cocked shotgun, immediately followed by the unmistakable feeling of the gun barrel pressed against my back...

TRUE STORY, AND THAT wasn't even the day I quit *that* job. I'll tell you the whole story later, but suffice to say, that was an especially hard day on the job.

Over the course of my career spanning more than forty years, I've certainly had my fair share of tough days on the job—some more nerve-wracking than others, and thankfully, only one that involved a shotgun. Now that I've reached this point in my professional journey, I can't help but look back at the many situations I've encountered and the many lessons I've learned, and as I do so, I am reminded of the amazing people who helped me along the way.

When I say "amazing," I mean it. I have worked with and learned from some of the absolute finest and most talented people in their fields, people who cared enough to take the time to teach me, to mentor me, to coach me into being a better employee, a better leader, and ultimately, a better version of myself. There have been many, but one man looms large in my memory, Homer Evans. Homer Evans is a legend at Hallmark. He spent his entire thirty-eight-year business career there, profoundly impacting the professional and personal lives of hundreds, maybe thousands. He was demanding, but I learned more from him in the two short years I worked for him than I did in the five years before or after.

In 1989, I was tasked with presenting at our national sales meeting—twenty-one, ninety-minute presentations over the span of twelve days. Homer, who *must* have had better things to do than sit through my spiel, sat through every single one of my twenty-one presentations, and after every single one, he provided concise and direct feedback on how I could improve for the next presentation. He did it in such a way that I knew he wasn't being critical. He was truly investing his time in helping me do a better job, and because of his help, each presentation was better than the one before. He even went as far as to stay through the final presentation, and true to form, approached me afterward with his recommendations written on a three by five notecard. When I explained that that was the last one, he replied, "Well, you still need to know," and he launched into his review of what I could do differently, what I should have said, what I shouldn't have, etc.

Not too terribly long ago, Homer paid me an unexpected visit on a Sunday afternoon. I hadn't seen him in many years, but I had reached out to him after my first book was published. I sent him a copy and thanked him for his commitment to me so early on in my fledgling career. I sent copies and similar thank-you's to many people who had influenced me, and strangely enough, I heard back from all but two—Homer being one of them. I was disappointed I hadn't heard from him. His opinion meant a great deal to me and I was hoping for *something*; a note, an email, a phone call. Nothing. That is, until that surprise afternoon visit to my home.

Decked out in his Sunday finest and eighty-seven years young, he shook my hand and said, "A couple weeks ago, I received a copy of your book in the mail, and I read it cover to cover. In fact, I read it several times, and I just came here to tell you person to person, man to man, that I think you did a superior job. I'm very proud of you for trying to reach out to others to help them, and I wanted to tell you thank you and good job."

We chatted for ten minutes or so, and then he explained he was a busy man and had many other things on his agenda for the day, so he headed for the door. I watched him as he took careful steps toward his pristine vehicle and got inside. He put his hands firmly at ten and two, adjusted his rear-view mirror, and drove away. I never saw him again. Homer passed away in June of 2017.

That visit was truly a watershed moment in my life. I couldn't believe he went to all the trouble to come see me face to face. He didn't have to do that. I looked up to Homer so much. The thought that he would make a special trip just to see me was mind boggling. That was him though, always going above and beyond.

Ironically, the other mentor from my past whom I had not heard back from reached out to me later that same Sunday. His name is Lanny Julian. Lanny was in sales—he could charm the pants right off just about anyone, but he possessed the intellect to back up his claims and was ahead of his time in his thinking and approach to business. Back in the eighties, he was working on an ethnic business center for Hallmark, looking at the ways we market and sell to various ethnic groups. Although commonplace now, back then, it was an innovative approach.

Anyway, as I was still basking in the glow of Homer's unexpected visit, I received a message on Facebook from Lanny. He told me he was proud of me and had always believed in me. I had just lamented to my wife earlier that morning how dejected I felt about not hearing from Homer or Lanny; now, here they both were on the same day, offering words of praise and encouragement. I was floored.

Homer and Lanny's influences, along with those of so many others like them, are truly my impetus for writing this book. I was so fortunate in my career to have these people in my corner, I feel a responsibility to pay that forward. I sincerely want to help those coming after me, to give them something tangible, something valuable, like I was given, something to help anyone who is aspiring to success and seeking the knowledge to achieve it.

Like everyone, I've made my fair share of mistakes throughout the years, and it was almost always the mistakes that provided the most valuable insights, gave me the most memorable experiences, and taught me the lessons that helped shape me into the leader I strive to be today. I want to share some of those lessons with you, and I promise not to sugarcoat the mistakes. My hope is that I can help you avoid those same mistakes, to reroute around the potholes I've encountered during my career.

I also do not want to leave you with the impression that this road has been easy because nothing is farther from the truth. Your path to leadership will trip you up many times and keep you on your toes. Success in business is hard. Life is hard, but every single day, we have a choice. Just because something is hard doesn't mean it's not worth trying or working for. I want to help younger professionals embrace this reality—yes, it's hard, but do it anyway.

If you're reading this book, you probably already know that leadership is not easy. Maybe you already are a leader who is seeking ways to improve, or perhaps you're a manager aspiring to become a leader, or maybe you're an individual contributor looking for ways to learn and grow. In any case, to become a leader, you must distinguish yourself from all the other hard-charging hopefuls around you. What constitutes a strong leader is the willingness to continually learn, to allow yourself to be coached, and the ability to avoid making the same mistakes repeatedly. You have to set the vision, weather the storm, and stay the course. This is challenging, but if you have some kind of framework or structure to guide you, a set of principles to fall back on, you can and will be successful. In sharing my set of guiding principles —my leadership philosophy—with you, I hope you can begin to flesh that out for yourself.

Perhaps my *most* important reason for writing this book is to leave something behind for my four children and grandchildren. They know and love me as "Dad" and "Papi," but I wanted to give them a glimpse into the side of me they never see. I wanted them to know some of the people and stories that shaped me and my career. I wanted to share the lessons I have learned with them, and at the end of the day, isn't that what really matters?

Regardless of where you work or what your title is, none of it means anything without the people who love you. As you strive for future success, keep in mind the things that matter and the reasons you work in the first place, and remember that far more important than being a leader at the office is the person you are when you go home.

Part One

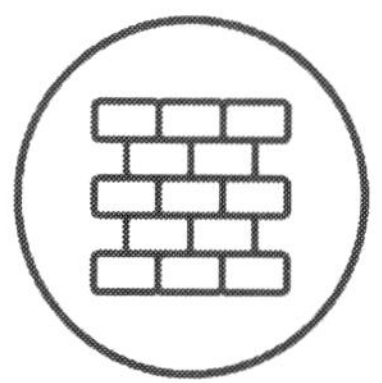

BUILD FROM THE GROUND UP

Where we come from, how we were raised,
our backgrounds, our previous experiences—
these factors play an important role in who we are,
how we see the world, and the manner in which
we conduct business and lead others.
There is considerable value in identifying who and
what has influenced you and understanding
the ways your past impacts your day to day dealings.
When putting together your leadership philosophy,
start from the beginning.
I began by asking myself why it was important
to have a leadership philosophy at all.
Then, I spent some time reflecting on my upbringing,
the people who shaped and encouraged me,
and the lessons I learned early in my career.

Chapter 1

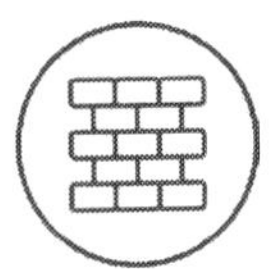

Why Have a Philosophy?

After graduating from the University of Arkansas with both bachelor's and master's degrees in Business, I was offered a job with Hallmark Cards, Inc., a job that piqued my interest, but one I declined because I had already accepted a position with a freight company. I felt obligated to give that job a chance since I had committed to it first, but after only eight months, I knew it was not a good fit for me. I went back to Hallmark and accepted the position—been there ever since.

I spent seven years in field assignments before moving to a corporate position at Hallmark's headquarters in Kansas City, which was the beginning of my path toward leadership. I learned from the examples of the strong leaders above me and around me in other divisions. I knew they were good leaders not only because of how they conducted themselves and led their businesses to success year after year, but also because they took the time to work with the people who reported to them, people like me, to nurture them into the next generation of leaders who would keep the company growing and thriving for many years to come.

I have been at Hallmark for the last thirty-eight years, most of that time in the sales division, working with Hallmark's largest customers:

Walmart, Sam's, Safeway, Publix, Kmart, Target, Toys R Us, Kroger, Stop & Shop, Amazon, Asda in the U.K., and Alibaba in China. I have also worked with an impressive group of owners who run our specialty Hallmark Gold Crown Stores. I have held a myriad of roles and titles and spent the last twenty-five years in key leadership positions. At one point, I led an organization of over five thousand people, and at another, I led an organization of over nine thousand people. The only reason I mention any of this is to demonstrate that I've held numerous leadership positions across a wide range of businesses for quite some time. I've learned a lot, made many mistakes, and although I consider myself to be very much a work still in progress, I believe that I have some valuable lessons and insights to pass along.

One of the biggest lessons I've learned, and one that took me years to understand and develop, is that the most effective leaders conduct their day-to-day decisions and interactions based on a set of principles that they have worked to internalize and implement over years of experience. This set of principles is what I have come to know as a "leadership philosophy," and the longer I have been a leader, the more convinced I have become of its absolute necessity for success.

> *Predictability provides a base upon which to make decisions that your team will act on quickly and without hesitation because over time, you have earned their trust.*

A leadership philosophy is important because strong leaders are consistent and prove themselves reliable over time. Strong leaders are predictable leaders. They are predictable in their actions, their expectations of others, and their decision making. The team you lead should know what you expect from them every day and what's important to you. Your team should know how you want to work, what you consider distracting to the business, and what you consider to be dysfunctional. Your team should know, with as much clarity as possible, how you want to get the job done.

Strong leadership demands this level of predictability because predictability creates a solid foundation of trust. Predictability overcomes misperceptions and false impressions people might otherwise develop about their leader. Predictability provides a base upon which to make decisions that your team will act on quickly and without hesitation because over time, you have earned their trust.

Consider the opposite of "predictability." Where there is no predictability, there is mayhem and guesswork. Ultimately, that results in a great amount of re-work, along with wasted time and misappropriated resources. It can be quite demoralizing to an organization when a leader is unpredictable. When a leader is predictable, it allows everyone on the team to feel empowered, secure, and engaged in the work that needs to be done.

A leadership philosophy provides you, the leader, with a set of guiding principles to help you navigate the waters and stay the course. It provides a structured framework to fall back on when things get crazy or go off the rails. Even if you're a newcomer to the business world, you already know that things *will* go off the rails. It's true in life and certainly true in business—you can count on the fact that things aren't always going to go the way you planned or projected. It is during those times that having a leadership philosophy becomes even more crucial because that is what can help you get back on track. Think of it like a compass or a north star. It's always there and it's always useful, but it can be an absolute life saver when you're lost.

It is important to realize that a leadership philosophy is an individual's set of beliefs. It does not necessarily represent the company's beliefs and values. It does not necessarily represent the division you work for. It's not a business plan or an operating plan. It's a set of personal guidelines you determine, based on your own unique experiences and perspectives, that you decide to follow yourself. It defines how *you* want to work.

If you have established the necessary credibility and predictability, they will trust your leadership, they will know how to work with you, and they will be able to move forward with confidence.

When I was working on drafting my leadership philosophy several years ago, I visited with my executive coach on multiple occasions. I kept asking her, "What do you think?"

She consistently responded, "What do *you* think?"

This back and forth happened several more times before I finally answered, "*I* think it's great!"

She smiled, "Then, you got it!"

It's *your* leadership philosophy, yours and yours alone, and it can become the handbook your team uses to figure out how to spend their time working on the problems they need to solve. If your team knows your expectations, they can act without having to check with you every time they make a decision. If you have established the necessary credibility and predictability, they will trust your leadership, they will know how to work with you, and they will be able to move forward with confidence.

Too many times, I've seen teams that do not know how to work with their leader. Nowadays, when many of us are being asked to accomplish more with fewer resources every single day of every single year, the inefficiency that results from not knowing how to work with your leader is no longer acceptable. There simply is no slack in the rope for inefficiency, for time to pass waiting on decisions to be made, for redundant checks and balances. There is no more room in the professional world for a team to not know how to work with their leader, and as the leader, it's your job to make certain this does not happen.

A leadership philosophy is alive. It grows and changes. My philosophy evolves a little each year. I revise and add pieces to it all the time. I reevaluate it constantly as I change with the changing times. I reshape it a bit every time I experience something different, every time I learn something new.

It's particularly important in our world today to be able to rethink your leadership philosophy because the day-to-day actions of a leader have changed more rapidly in recent years. Fifteen years ago, when I started to work on my leadership philosophy, there was no text messaging, no Instagram, no Facebook, no LinkedIn. There will always be new methods of communication, and so leaders must always be willing to change the methods they use to communicate with their teams. As all of us get older and bring new talent onto our teams, maybe some younger talent, we've got to make sure the techniques we use to implement our leadership philosophy and the methods we use to communicate it are acceptable to everyone on our teams. While the newer talent needs to adapt to the leader's philosophy, the leader must also adapt to changing technologies and changing teams and the way they want to work.

The way I work with my team today, as a veteran leader, is vastly different than what it was when I ran my first team, and I know that each and every one of the changes I've made has been absolutely necessary. It doesn't matter if I like a change I've decided to make or not. It doesn't matter what my personal preferences are. I look at how the times are changing and I change with them. I look at my new choices, and I pick the methods that work for me and my team as it exists in that time and place.

For the last twenty-nine months, I have led several virtual teams composed of talented individuals from across the company. None of them are direct reports—all of them have their own roles within the company but are giving me time throughout the week to work on special assignments. I have thoroughly enjoyed the opportunity to work on a broad array of interesting initiatives, and while working with these various virtual teams, I've noticed something. A strong leadership philosophy is effective even when you're working with people who are *not* direct reports. I've been able to implement every single element of my philosophy with my virtual teams, and it works!

In this book, I want to share my leadership philosophy with you. I'm not trying to convince you that my leadership philosophy should be yours. I only want to give you an example of what a leadership philosophy looks like. I'll explain how I came to develop it through some of the experiences I've had in the working world, and I'll demonstrate how I've put my philosophy to use and how it has worked for me over the course of my career.

For Reflection

You probably already have a few guiding principles that help you navigate your personal and professional life, even if you have not previously identified those as a leadership philosophy. Think about those principles...off the top of your head, list three to five. Which one would you consider the most important? Explain why.

Chapter 2

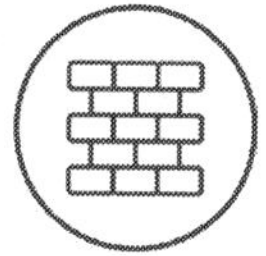

An Early Gift

I GREW UP IN southern Arkansas in the small town of El Dorado. My mother was one of ten children, my father was one of eight, and both grew up in poverty. Both of my parents worked and neither finished high school.

My father's father was a bridge builder near the turn of the twentieth century, back in the days when there was very little equipment and safety gear. It was hard manual labor and considered extremely dangerous. My mother's parents worked miscellaneous jobs, one of which was to wash clothes for the military troops at Camp Robinson during World War II. They lived the kind of lives where working hard was not an option because they needed every next dollar they earned to survive.

My dad was an auto mechanic for his entire career, and my mother operated a press machine for a printing company. My dad drove a company truck because there were many times during the evenings and weekends when he would get a call requiring him to drive to the site of a broken-down vehicle. I remember always having that company mechanic's truck parked out in front of our house.

My dad was also a World War II combat veteran. Because he refused to leave behind a wounded friend, he was captured by German soldiers and spent more than a year as a prisoner of war. He was awarded a Purple Heart, and I believe, a Silver Star, although I have not been able to verify this. He never really talked about his time over there. He returned from the war before I was even born, so I never saw him as a soldier. During my childhood, there were many TV shows chronicling military adventures during World War II – shows like *Combat*, *Hogan's Heroes*, and *Twelve O'Clock High*. When those shows came on, my dad always left the room. He said there was nothing to be entertained by there, nothing to celebrate. He didn't think people should be making money off something so horrendous. He said it was not something to be proud of.

Along with his daily job fixing cars for the garage, my dad also worked on cars for people on his own, mainly through our church. People brought their cars over at night and he changed the oil or the brake pads or the plugs or the points, whatever was needed. Often, he bartered for services. He fixed the car for the guy who fixed our radio and TV. He worked on the car for a carpenter who would fix things around our house. He regularly worked on the car for the guy who was our plumber. Also, there were folks who had big gardens or herds of livestock, so people sometimes paid for their car repairs with vegetables and meats. It was an unsophisticated, but successful bartering system that our community had in place, and most of the time, it worked out evenly, but no one really cared when it didn't.

He always told me, "Get a job where you don't get dirty."

My father was a simple man, and I remember having a very simple childhood. A good day for my dad was watching the Arkansas Razorbacks win a football game on Saturday or the Cowboys win on Sunday. If he had a nice meal to eat and a tall glass of sweet tea, he was a happy man.

He was in the church choir, and if they sang his favorite song during the service, "In the Garden," then it was truly a perfect day.

I'm sure it's clear by now that we never had much money, although it was always a topic of conversation in our house. We talked about money when we had it, and we talked about it when we didn't. Anytime we saw something new or interesting, my dad would speculate aloud, "I wonder how much that cost?" I remember we collected S&H Green Stamps, and every six months, we'd all sit at the dining room table pasting those stamps into books that would only amount to a few dollars, but every little bit helped.

My dad liked to reference a man he knew from church named Bob who owned his own little drug store. I bet I heard my dad say a hundred times, "Son, you need to grow up to be like Bob. He probably makes ten or twelve thousand dollars a year, and he never gets dirty."

I think my dad felt badly that he came home dirty. He perpetually smelled of gasoline and oil, and his hands were always dirty the way a workingman's hands would be. The only soap we had in the whole house was Lava, a gritty pumice that was supposed to clean everything from greasy grime to sticky glue and paint, but even Lava never quite got my dad's hands completely clean. There was always some stain left behind. This was a key point for him. He always told me, "Get a job where you don't get dirty."

While the other kids in my small town were learning trade skills from their parents – how to fix cars or do plumbing or carpentry work, my dad did not have any desire to teach me his craft. Many nights, hundreds of nights, I accompanied him to the shop because he needed to put a car on the lift or needed some of the larger equipment to complete a nighttime repair job. I watched him work and often asked, "Dad, can you show me how to do that?"

I wanted to learn how to put on the brake pads, change the oil, change the fan belt, or set the timing, anything. It all looked so interesting. His response was always the same, "Go into the office and study."

The office was just a small, dirty room with a phone and a desk pushed up against the wall. The desk was grimy and spotted with oil, but I'd clear a space and study, just like he told me to do. Maybe we'd have the Cardinals on the radio, and I'd sit there and try to study, but my mind would often wander or I'd get bored. I'd walk back over to him and ask him to show me what he was doing.

He was adamant, "I don't want you doing this. If I teach you how to do this, then someday you'll have an old car out under a shade tree in the back yard that you're working on, and pretty soon, you'll buy another car that you're going to fix up to sell, and before long you'll be in debt, and then you'll find a girl and you'll get married, and you'll end up being me. I don't want you to be me. I want you to be somebody different than me. I want you to be like Bob. I want you to go be the best you can be."

At one point, when I considered going into the ministry, I vividly remember broaching the subject with my dad. I was very active in my church as a kid and involved in some statewide church activities, so it made sense that I thought I might have a calling there.

When I told him, he replied, "Don't do that, you're not going to make any money if you do that. If you want to go to church, then go to church. If you want to influence people there, then do that, but you're not going to go into the ministry." He really put his foot down. He continued, "You can go to church anytime you want to, but you need to get a job that allows you to take care of your family."

I listened when my parents talked about money, when my dad told me to get a job where I didn't get dirty, and when he told me not to be like my older brother who never finished high school. I listened, I finished high school, and I went on to the University of Arkansas in Fayetteville. I chose it because it only cost two hundred and five dollars a semester in the fall of 1974 when I started, but also, and more importantly, because I was a huge Razorbacks fan. As a child, I attended one Razorbacks game every year with my dad and had such fond memories of those times.

I found that the work I did outside the classroom was what gave me the skills, the confidence, and the focus I needed to succeed, and that was just as useful to me, if not more so, than what all those other folks learned at their high-end universities.

The University of Arkansas was a terrific school for me. They had more than enough academic programs for me to choose from, and after a bit of a rocky first year-and-a-half, I buckled down and started earning good grades. I went straight into graduate school there, studied year-round right through the summer, and finished my MBA, much to the shock of my parents. I don't think my dad ever got his arms around the fact that I was going to be making more than ten or twelve thousand dollars a year at any point in my life.

As surprised as they may have been, I always knew I had the support of my parents, and they did everything they could to help me. They didn't have any extra money, but somehow, they found a way to send me a hundred dollars every month while I was in school, which I know must have been a significant sacrifice for them. I had to figure out on my own how to make the rest of the money I needed to live, so I had to work. Because of that, I came to realize that what you do outside the classroom is as important to your success as what you do inside the classroom, and in some cases, even more so.

I *had* to work to pay rent and buy food. If I didn't, I wouldn't be able to eat and I wouldn't have a roof over my head. I had no other options. It was all on me. If I couldn't make it, I would've had to have gone home, and my life would've ended up looking exactly like my dad said it would. I was motivated by sheer survival.

Years later, as I progressed further in my career, I worked with people who went to prestigious colleges—Indiana, Harvard, Stanford, Northwestern—lots of great schools which were much more expensive than mine. I'm sure those schools provided a great education, but as I moved up and became a leader who was looking for talented people to work with me, I was more interested in what they had done during their college years when they were *not* in class. What activities did they take part in? Did they have to deliver on something outside the classroom that gave them some real-world experience? I found that the work I did outside the classroom was what gave me the skills, the confidence, and the focus I needed to succeed, and that was just as useful to me, if not more so, than what all those other folks learned at their high-end universities.

Not to say that those universities are not great. They most certainly are. If I had had the money and the opportunity, I would have loved to go to one of those schools, but looking back, I wouldn't trade an education like that for the balance of experience and education I received as a student at the University of Arkansas. The fact that I had to both study and earn a living, to make grades and make money, set me up for what I believe was the most important set of skills I would learn through the course of my entire career.

Clearly, the combination of experiences I had when I was young gave me the confidence to do what I've been doing, but the earliest and most important gift I received was from my dad. When I asked him to teach me how to change oil and rotate tires and change out brake pads, he said, "No." That set me on a path that I could have only dreamed possible.

When I got out of graduate school and started working on my first assignment or two, I saw so many people who were torqued by the choices they were making because their families were putting pressure on them to stay home, to stay near family, to learn the family business. Staying connected with family is obviously important, but my dad had a very different view about what it meant to do that. He told me, "You go be the best you can be. You'll eventually have a family and you will need to be able to take care of them. I'll be here. You call me. You'll see me when you come by. You write me a note. Just let me know you're doing okay. That's all I ask. You go be the best you can be."

That early gift is probably as important and as powerful as anything I learned in school or any work assignment I've had—the fact that I had permission from my father to leave and be the best that I could be. I got a good job, Dad, and I don't get dirty.

For Reflection

Think back to your childhood. What did you want to be when you grew up? Who were some of the people who influenced you? What was the most valuable advice you were given? What do you wish you would have known then that you know now?

Chapter 3

The Most Important Lesson

I CONSIDER MYSELF FORTUNATE to have worked at Hallmark for all these years and to have been able to work with Don Hall, Jr., the current CEO and grandson of the founder, Joyce Hall. He and I are roughly the same age, so in a sense, we "grew up" together in the company. I first met Don in November of 1987 when he taught me one of the most important lessons I have learned along my entire career path—*do the extra things that can lead to your success.*

I'll never forget that first encounter with him. Don was a product manager in our stationery business at the time, and I had been newly relocated to Kansas City. Don was going to help reset a product offering in a local Kansas City store, The Country Mouse, and he asked me to help him with the reset one night. This involved changing out the merchandizing shelves and placing new product and store signage, etc. This particular reset was a trial run for a new store configuration we planned to launch soon.

I was one of forty people who arrived at four o'clock in the afternoon to help with the reset. We immediately got to work. At eight o'clock, there were probably twenty people there, and by ten o'clock, there were nine or ten. One hour later, Don and I were the only ones left. At this point in my life, because I had just moved from Texas and my family had not yet joined me, I had no one waiting for me at home and nowhere else I had to be, so I thought I would just stay as long as Don stayed, no matter how late it got.

We continued to work into the night until we eventually finished and put everything away. I don't even remember what time it was, but I know it was late. I assumed we were done, until Don disappeared into the back-storage area of the store and re-emerging with a vacuum cleaner. He began vacuuming the entire store, which was probably a five thousand square foot space. Don, the grandson of the company's owner and future CEO, set out to vacuum every last inch of it!

I thought to myself again, "I'm going to stay here as long as this guy stays here. I'm just going to ride this thing out." I went into the back, located some glass cleaner and paper towels, and began dusting while Don vacuumed. We cleaned every surface in that store until the place was spotless. We even took out the trash, and then finally headed for the door.

Do the little things, whatever those things might be in your current situation.

I helped Don carry out some extra merchandising parts to load into his trunk. I had imagined that Joyce Hall's grandson drove some expensive car, but to my surprise, I followed him to a mid-seventies Toyota sedan (or something like that). I noticed there were bits and pieces of merchandising parts and boxes of stationery piled in the back, and to be honest, it was really kind of a mess with all the fixtures and product. I found this interesting and certainly not what I expected.

I headed to my hotel around two in the morning and back to the office by seven for a meeting at seven-thirty. I was in my little cube with my cup of coffee when Don walked by, also up bright and early for his next meeting. He stopped at my desk and said, "Hey Wayne, thanks for coming out last night. We got a lot of good work done and I appreciate your help."

It was then that I realized these people were special. If the person who was one day going to be the CEO was out there in the field grinding it out when he didn't have to, then there was something remarkable about this company.

Do the little things, whatever those things might be in your current situation. As a sales person, your little thing might be to make one extra sales call before you go to lunch or before you leave at the end of the day. Think about whatever the equivalent of that is in your job and make the effort to do it. You know what those things look like—do them even if nobody notices that you're doing them because it isn't about getting credit. It's about taking the actions at every point in your career that can further your success. Going the extra mile is a lesson that has informed my actions and decisions ever since that late-night store reset, a lesson I learned by sheer example, and one that has made all the difference.

For Reflection

We are constantly learning. What are some of the lessons you learned early in your career? If you could pass along only ONE lesson to someone just starting out in the workforce, what would it be, and why?

Part Two

My Leadership Philosophy

My philosophy of leadership is rooted in four essential principles: communication, courage, clarity, and conviction. These principles guide my thinking and shape my behaviors, helping me to be consistent and predictable in the ways I conduct myself and my team. These principles steer my every move and create a solid framework for the various elements that make up my leadership philosophy.

Communication

I begin with "Communication" because it is fundamental for success. Much of what a good leader does day to day involves open, honest, and sometimes even courageous communication. It is imperative for leaders to communicate up front who they are, what they need, what they expect, and how they want to work. It is equally important to cultivate excellent listening skills and a keen awareness of when to speak and when to remain silent.

CHAPTER 4

GET TO KNOW YOUR TEAM AND LET THEM GET TO KNOW YOU

TWENTY YEARS AGO, I was assigned to a new leader—a woman who had been very successful before joining our company. By the time I met her, she had been running a product division at Hallmark for several years and was asked to head the division that served our largest retailer. Once I got to know her, I asked her how she had been able to achieve so much success running different businesses that she really knew nothing about at the onset of those various assignments.

She assured me that it was not that difficult to get started. She always met with the top customers she was newly assigned to and asked them three questions:

1. What are we doing well?
2. What should we stop doing?
3. If you were me, what would you start doing?

After meeting with those top customers, several trends would emerge. These were influential, experienced retailers who were not afraid to speak their minds, and so they were happy to make it clear what they liked us doing, what they wanted us to stop doing, and what they wanted us to start working on. For the first year in that new assignment, she would focus on those issues, and over the course of that year, she would uncover new issues as well as new opportunities. She had early success in her new assignments because she simply did what her customers asked her to do. This sounds very simple, but a surprising number of new leaders fail to do this. They come into a new assignment with their own ideas and assumptions, their own agendas. They think they're doing what's best, but their results over that first year are often haphazard, revealing that their ideas and assumption may not have been entirely accurate.

Take the time to get to know your people at the start.

I adopted a version of her technique, and I use it every time I start with a new team. When I take on an assignment, one of the first things I do is devote at least an hour, maybe an hour-and-a-half, to each person on my team, one-on-one. Sometimes we go to lunch or have coffee. I try to create a relaxed, casual environment, and I simply ask them about themselves. I ask where they grew up and where they went to school. If they mention their family, I ask to hear more about them. I also ask, "What do you do for fun? What vacations have you taken recently? What are your hobbies?"

It's amazing what you will find out about your new team if you just ask questions. I've found out that some of my team were amazing musicians. I had one team member who was a track star in college. Another told me he had bowled six perfect games. I've had people who were active in their church or in the community, people who were members of the Junior League. Take the time to get to know your people at the start.

In addition to personal details, an important question to ask is this, "What are the three things you did best in your last assignment, and in the assignment before that?" If you know more about their work performance than just what's going on in the present, you will find that you can reach them and have a better relationship with them. You will be better able to leverage their talents, have personal conversations with them during tough times, and you will make them feel like the valued and dignified team members they are.

Knowing something team members value outside of work, something they feel good about, has helped me many times. If I notice someone is having a frustrating day or is feeling stuck on an assignment, I might be able to say something like, "Hey, how's the bowling going?" or "How's your old college track team doing this year?" If I can get someone's mind off their frustration for a moment, but also remind them of something that excites them and that they're good at, they might regain a bit of the confidence they need to get through the rest of that day or to re-engage in their project.

At the end of our meeting together, I always ask the same questions I learned from my boss twenty years ago, "If you were me, what would you continue to do? What would you stop doing? And what would you start doing that isn't happening yet?"

Just as when you ask your customers these questions, the same thing will happen with your team. Four or five trends will emerge, one of them likely being how they feel about leadership's communication style. Many people will say they are looking for ways to understand our strategy better. Another might be a common opinion about how objectives are set.

As the leader of a new organization, if you address those issues quickly with your team, if you say, "I hear we need to start working on this," or "I heard from a lot of you that we need to stop doing this, so we're going to stop doing it," your team will feel like they have been heard, like their opinions matter, and they will feel motivated and empowered.

If you can do this within your first sixty to ninety days as the leader of a new organization, and communicate back to your team, "We heard you, we're going to take this action now," and if you show that you've taken an interest in them as people, you and your team will get off to an incredibly fast and effective start. Make this a priority as a first step. You'll see trends that you can address right away to speed up the process, and your new team members will then naturally want to get to know more about you.

It's also important in the first ninety days to "clean up" any unresolved issues left behind by the previous leader. In my experience, when you take on a new team, you always inherit a set of prior crises that need addressing. This requires a leader to be patient and deliberate, but handling these things early on will propel your team farther and faster in the long run.

The next thing I do is set up thirty to forty-five minutes to meet one-on-one with the people who report to the people who report to me. Even when I've led very large organizations, I've taken the time to meet with as many as a hundred people. Looking back, that may have been too many, but spending time with fifteen, twenty, thirty people, even if it's just a half-hour or so, and getting to know them is imperative. It can make all the difference in how much more willing they might be to align themselves with your leadership style.

In my mid-thirties, I was vice president of marketing for our Hallmark Gold Crown stores, and I had a strong relationship with the woman who had been running the team. We had settled into a smooth and comfortable routine involving the way she ran the team and how she wanted to work. One day, she told us she was leaving the company to pursue a career in education. About a week later, we were introduced to our new manager, a Harvard graduate who had worked at Gillette before coming to Hallmark. Since coming to Hallmark, she had successfully run a couple of very large divisions before taking this new position leading a sizeable customer team. She was extremely intelligent, incredibly focused, and extraordinarily intimidating.

During the first thirty days, everyone on the team struggled to get on the same page with her as it became clear how exceedingly different her work style was from that of our previous leader. Many of us have been in this situation when assigned a new boss. You get together with your coworkers around the building or after work and things are said like, "Why did she do this? Why did she do that? You won't believe what she asked me to do today!" You're sharing all these stories and before you know it, you've settled into a pattern of complaining. We've all been there.

This is where our team quickly found itself after only a few weeks with our new leader. It was tough for us. She left each of us five or six voicemails every day, dictating every move we should make and requiring that we spend a great deal of time detailing what we were spending our time on, focusing intently on "the monthly report." She had us spend a day or two getting our division monthly report exactly right before she turned it in. She was very good at managing upward, at using the efforts of her team to best communicate to her boss the successes she was leading. That is not necessarily a negative because she made certain that our CEO and president understood the resources we needed and the results that would come from having access to those resources. She could tell a compelling story to our leadership.

However, when each of us met with her one-on-one, there was no room for chitchat. You were expected to walk into those meetings with an agenda and get through that agenda. She was acutely focused on the details of every project. After about a month of working for her, she asked me, "So, how are we doing, you and I?"

I had to be honest. I replied, "Well, half of the time I don't like working with you, and half of the time I'm undecided."

Like I mentioned, I was in my mid-thirties, and I had a great deal of bravado, perhaps more bravado than I had skills to back up at the time. Surprisingly, she didn't get mad at me. She said, "I can see that. I might have expected that, but we're going to do something in the next few weeks that I hope will change that."

A few weeks later, she gathered the team together. We were a fairly sizable team—ten or twelve people—each with very different functions: sales, marketing, HR, retail, and so forth. It was a diverse group of responsibilities she was called upon to oversee and a wide range of skill sets she had to pull together. We went to an offsite location owned by the Hall family, referred to simply as "The Farm," a comfortable farmhouse maybe twenty miles out of town that was used for corporate retreats. It sat on a large piece of property and had a relaxed atmosphere. She brought us all up there, sat us down, and started telling us her story.

She shared how she had grown up. She told us a little bit about her childhood and about her experiences in high school. She talked about her time at Harvard, which was intimidating to some of us with its highbrow reputation. I knew the tuition I had paid at the University of Arkansas probably wouldn't have even paid for her books at Harvard. She talked about her husband and her family and the time she spent working at Gillette. She was very honest about the successes she had during her time there, as well as some of the struggles she had faced. Throughout this sharing, we got to know her. She showed us her personality, her history, and by doing so, she gave us some insight into her leadership style and her decision-making process. We now knew the story behind her very tough exterior.

In the moment, I thought this was the most ridiculous waste of time I had ever sat through in my life. I had never heard anything like this before, and I had been doing this kind of work for a long time. I had never experienced this extensive sharing of personal information in a professional setting, especially by the leader of the group.

Ultimately, however, I changed my mind about that day we spent at The Farm. I ended up working for her for about three-and-a-half years, and as I look back on all the people I've worked for throughout my career, I learned more from her in those years than I did from any other leader. She was incredibly focused and a great teacher. She helped me to see the vital importance of communicating clearly with a team up front, letting them know who you are, why you're that way, and how you like to work. Taking the time to communicate in this way with new teams early on has saved me countless hours. When a team has insight into who you are and how you work, it cuts the guesswork out of everyone's jobs, allowing your team to focus on results and the real work at hand. For you, as a leader, it means you can concentrate on what you need to focus on rather than constantly harping on your team or redoing things the way you wanted them done in the first place. Invest the time up front and it will pay off in the long haul.

For Reflection

If you're not already in the habit of getting to know your team, make a list of three to five questions you could ask each of them. How comfortable are you sharing some of your personal life and background with your team? What are two personal details that your team may not know about you? What are three things you could share with your team about your background that would give them insight into how you work?

Chapter 5

Explain Your Nits

That day at The Farm, after my new boss shared her personal background with us, she then took us through what she called her "personal nits." By "nits," she meant the actions people on her team took, the methods of communication, the ways they spent their time, that bothered her. She said, "You may think these are odd, or silly, or that I should be able to move past them, but this is how I like to work, and the sooner you can get on the same page with me about how I like to work, the quicker you're going to get comfortable working with me, and the better able we will be to make our performance targets."

After listening to how she liked to work in such detail and understanding a bit about the reasons behind her preferences, I realized that the times I had been most frustrated working with her were the times I was giving her information in a way that was incongruent with how she liked to receive that information. I realized that I had, on several occasions, worked with her in ways she did not like to work. Those "nits," as she called them, have become an integral part of my leadership philosophy.

Now, every time I assemble a new team, I not only take the time to get to know them and let them know a little about me, I also walk them through what I've come to identify as my personal nits. One hundred percent of the time, the new people on my team love it. They appreciate knowing how I like the team to function, how I arrived at my preferences based on my past experiences, how I like to work with people individually, and what's important to me day to day in the office. Most of the people who have worked for me and eventually moved on to larger leadership positions use this method with their new teams, as well. I highly recommend you do, too, especially if you are a new leader, but even if you're an experienced leader who is starting out with a new team, you may find it helpful.

It is equally important to ask your team about their nits. It benefits everyone to define what the working relationship will look like, and it is just that—a relationship.

It is equally important to ask your team about their nits. It benefits everyone to define what the working relationship will look like, and it is just that—a relationship. It requires give and take, mutual understanding and respect, and certainly honesty. Be honest with your people about who you are and how you like to work, and encourage them to be honest with you in return.

To illustrate, I'm going to walk you through my nits and the reasons behind them. This is not to tell you that these should be your nits, but these examples of the things that irritate me might help you begin to think about what your nits are, what you would like your team to know about how you like to work and not work, so that all of you can function more effectively together.

Nit: Don't copy me on emails just to show me you're doing something. People complain all the time about the excessive number of emails they receive. I certainly don't want to read any more than I absolutely must, so I have given my team a barometer to help them determine whether or not an email needs to be sent. I tell them to ask themselves this question, "Does he need to know this?" If the answer is "no," then don't copy me.

Copying me on emails unnecessarily is a sign of professional immaturity. When a person feels like he/she needs to copy the boss on every email, it demonstrates a lack of experience and confidence, and I clearly communicate to my team that I feel this way. When I put it to my team like this, guess how many emails I get copied on from that day forward? I can assure you, very few. I think all of us have gone through periods in our careers when too many hours of our day were spent going through emails that were irrelevant to our responsibilities. They are useless, sometimes senseless in general, and can even be ridiculous.

Many times, people are simply trying to impress their managers, "Look at me! I'm working! Look at this really nice, long, thorough email I sent!" I tell my team that I assume they're working. If they're not working, I'm going to find out and it's going to lead to a different conversation. I'll know you're working if you're delivering on the results we're looking for and delivering them on time. Don't tell me you're working by copying me on emails.

Nit: Don't blind copy me on anything. Think about what the purpose of blind copying your boss would be. You're probably debating something with another person and you secretly want your boss to know about it because you'd like your boss's authority to be on *your* side. I tell my team that if they feel that way and think I need to be brought into the debate, respect the other person enough by being open about the fact that I've been brought in on the conversation. If you believe you're right, then have the courage to talk about it openly. When I receive an email that was sent to someone else and I have been blind copied, it just tells me that the sender lacks courage. If you think I should be copied on an email you're sending to someone else, then copy me, but do not ever blind copy me.

Nit: Never forward a voicemail I have sent to you. In today's world, people leave fewer voicemails, but I believe the same standard applies to text messages and emails. Don't forward the phone messages, text messages, or emails I have sent to you. The message was sent to *you* with a specific tone, with specific language, with specific information that you and I share between us based on our history of working together. That message was not intended to be shared with other people.

When someone forwards a message of any kind, it can cause problems. It may be interpreted in any number of different ways by different people, and if the chain of communication starts to lengthen, if the message gets forwarded on beyond one person, then the intent of the message has an even higher risk of misinterpretation. If I have a straightforward approach with one person, another person may think I was angry with the intended recipient, when in fact, that is just the tone I take because I know that person well enough to get to the point. Someone not directly intended to see that email may read some undertone into it that is not intended to be there.

As a leader, you don't have time to clean up language and craft communication which is intended to be seen by your team, by the people who know you, out of concern that it may be seen by everyone else in the corporation. Your team members need to understand this and not forward your fast-moving communications. If I have confidence that my team members will not do this, then I can communicate quickly and move on, allowing progress to continue efficiently on that issue.

Nit: Never surprise me. If we have an issue, if one of my people discovers a problem, then they need to find me, call me, come by my

It's been my experience that if you can get the right people involved as soon as you know there's a problem, you can deal with it sooner and navigate to a better solution.

office, sit down with me, and say, "We've got a problem." You can't surprise me with bad news that you've known about for a while in the hopes that you could fix it without me ever knowing, and you really shouldn't surprise me with overwhelmingly good news either. If you're working on something big, let me know! Maybe I can help steer you toward an even better solution.

If there's a problem you've been made aware of in the business you're managing, or if you have an issue with how I'm handling something, tell me. As soon as you know there's a relevant problem, find me and communicate it to me. It's been my experience that if you can get the right people involved as soon as you know there's a problem, you can deal with it sooner and navigate to a better solution. The problem is often not as bad as the person who is closest to it might think, and there's almost always a way to solve it, but your leaders cannot help you if they find out too late. I encourage my team to have the courage and confidence to talk to me and trust our relationship enough to know that we can work it out together.

About fifteen to twenty years ago, I managed marketing, merchandizing, and oversaw a broad range of responsibilities for a group of retail stores. We were having a good year. It wasn't a perfect year, but it was a good year. At the beginning of December, we were all watching our revenue numbers come in and looking over our expenses. By the second week of December, we started to call out our budgets, seeing where we were compared to where we were supposed to be. I remember going into a room and asking a question about a particular marketing initiative, about where the team thought they were going to come in against their budget. I was looking for a very specific number. They gave me a number that was very close, and I left, feeling good about it.

In the third week of January, the actual numbers came in, and I received a half-a-million-dollar surprise. There were five hundred thousand dollars spent on a line in my budget that until that moment, I did not know about. I worked for a very strong leader at the time who called me almost immediately, just as I knew she would, and said, "I want to see you right now."

Sweating, I walked quickly down to her office. She laid the report down on her desk, looked me square in the eye, and said, "Tell me one thing. Did you know about this in December?"

"No, I did not," I replied. "I just found out now. I'm accountable for it, and I've already got a meeting scheduled this afternoon to bring the people managing this together, and I'll have an answer for you by the end of the day about how it happened."

"That's okay," she assured me. "I know you'll do all that. I just wanted to know if you knew about this before I did."

That surprise taught me this important lesson. If I had known about the problem back in December and not told her because I was fearful of her reaction or perception of me, I would have missed the chance for her to help me fix it. Not telling her would have cost me my job right then and there. Luckily, I did not know about it, and she trusted me, but I'll never forget that experience. I want my team to keep me in the loop—if I know what's going on, then I can do something about it.

Nit: Frequent communication with me is great, but you don't get extra credit for length. There are people who believe that the best communication in business is an essay or short story. It's a small book. They want to take every opportunity to demonstrate all the skills they learned in college about how to write a very effective piece of communication. That does not work for me. I like simple, direct, straightforward communication. I'm okay with frequent communication if it's relevant, necessary, timely, and certainly if it's urgent, but keep it concise and to the point.

If I receive a lengthy email that rambles on, or if I open a document and have to scroll down the page to find the information I need, I reply by saying I'm not going to read it. I explain that it's too long and I ask the sender to resend just the points that are relevant to me.

Usually, I only need to do this once for someone to catch on that I am serious about it. Typically, I immediately receive an email containing just the information relevant to me. I stop getting lengthy emails from those people from that point forward and instead receive quick, concise bullets of the information I need, presented to me in a way that allows me to find the necessary information quickly so I can get on with my day.

The same holds true for me with voicemails. If someone on my team leaves me a voicemail, they know they can ask me up to two questions. Once they have asked me two questions, I want them to hang up, even if they have to call back and leave me another voicemail. We've all gotten voicemails that start out with something like, "Hey, there! I haven't seen you in a while. How are you doing? Have you been to a baseball game yet this season? We're really on a streak right now," and so on.

They start off by getting chummy, and then they say, "There are three or four things I want to ask you." They begin with the first lengthy question, then the second, then the third, and by that point, I don't remember what the first question was. I tell people that if they want me to respond to something through voicemail, they need to keep it short. If the message goes on for longer than those two questions, I find myself having to rewind and play it back to hear things over again, and that's a waste of time.

Nit: Never complain to me about another person on my staff. If you're a person on my staff and you've got a problem with someone else, go talk to that person and work it out. You don't need to tell me that someone on my team is underperforming or not delivering because chances are good that I already know.

When I was in maybe my second or third leadership position, I had about ten or twelve managers reporting to me, each with significant responsibilities and several people working under them. One of the operations people constantly complained about a national accounts manager. The complaints were about how this accounts manager never provided information on time or was always changing the information and revising forecasts. The information that Operations was receiving was never correct.

If you are relatively young in your career or new to a company, you must discipline yourself to stay focused on your day-to-day responsibilities and hold yourself accountable to your deadlines.

The national accounts manager would then come in and tell me that the operations people were too demanding, that they were not flexible enough, and that they were unrealistically rigid because they didn't understand the marketplace. The first couple of times this happened, I told them both, "You have to work this out between yourselves."

The third time one of them complained about the other, I brought them both into my office, sat them down, and told them that the three of us were going to have a conversation. I looked at one of them and said, "You've got one minute to tell the other person what's going on.

Don't tell me, tell him. After one minute, I'm cutting you off. The other person has to sit quietly and listen. Then that person will have a minute to talk. Then the first person can respond for one minute."

After several rounds of going back and forth, the conversation slowed and eventually came to a grinding halt as it became clear they were getting nowhere. They were both clearly embarrassed. They started to understand that they were simply not communicating well with each other and that they could resolve this between themselves. They had gone back and forth for about ten minutes, doing nothing but waste my time, but they never came back to me to complain about each other ever again.

I don't like hearing complaints from my people about others on my team. It breeds negativity, and it causes team dysfunction. If someone comes into my office and complains, and other people hear about it, they may begin to believe I'm playing favorites. Whatever people may think about what's going on in that sort of situation, the outcome is never positive, so I never allow it. Period.

Nit: Don't make your lack of planning my crisis. If I have communicated to my team how I believe it should operate and the expectations I have for timely compliance, then they should know how much of a priority to make certain assignments. If you didn't plan well enough to get something done on time or didn't allow for the amount of time it takes for proper workflow, it's not my problem. Go figure it out.

Every company deals with individuals who have failed to properly plan and execute a project. Even otherwise high potential people can sometimes allow themselves to fall into this sort of complacent behavior. If you are relatively young in your career or new to a company, you must discipline yourself to stay focused on your day-to-day responsibilities and hold yourself accountable to your deadlines. Do quality work, and do it on time. Only by consistent successes at the execution level will you demonstrate your potential to one day take the reins of leadership yourself.

Do remember that everyone has made mistakes along the course of their careers, myself included, and very few mistakes are not recoverable. Calm accountability and a clear demonstration that you have learned from your mistakes is the best way to move forward—and don't make that same mistake twice.

That is what turns out to be my rather long list of personal nits. Again, I do not believe they need to be yours. I would never suggest that someone else take on my list of nits. This is very personal, and everyone is different. You will develop your own as you grow as a leader and run into all sorts of barriers to your team's productivity. I've heard leaders say they expect their people to sometimes work on weekends or at night. Some leaders like to answer emails at five o'clock in the morning. The point here is this: meet with your team. Have the courage to tell them whatever your work style and organizational expectations are. Communicate to them what's important to you so that you can give them the tools to be able to work with you effectively. Everyone wins in the end when you, the leader, do this.

For Reflection

We all have "nits." Give it some serious thought and write down five to seven. Then, explain why each of those are "nits" for you. Be honest.

Chapter 6

Define Expectations

In addition to frustrating work behaviors that can block the path to meeting our goals, I also have definite expectations of positive behaviors that I clearly communicate to my team at the onset. Just as with my "nits," I am not suggesting that my expectations be yours, but hopefully reading mine will jumpstart you on your way to defining what it is you expect from your team.

Expectation: When we have one-on-one time, spend it asking me questions. You're working on a project. You're facing some hurdles. I want you to tell me not only what those hurdles are, but what your options are for overcoming them. I want you to be able to tell me, "Here are possible solutions, A, B, and C. Here are the advantages to each of these solutions; here are the disadvantages." Then, ask me what I think. Ask me, "What am I missing? What have I not thought of? Who do you know who can help me?"

I want my team to use me for my insight, to draw upon my experience to help them decide which way to go. I want them to spend our one-on-one time focused on how they can use me to help them run their business. I do not want to spend my time talking about their travel schedules, their budgets, everything they did last week, all the things they're going to do next week, or over the next month. I don't need to know that. Again, I assume they're working. I don't need them to prove that to me.

What I *do* want to know are the key problems they're trying to sort through and how I can help sort through them. Maybe I've got some ideas they haven't thought of or perhaps I know someone who does, but I will not solve the problem for them. I *will* give them my take on the positives and negatives, and then I expect them to go figure it out.

Expectation: Use the time we have together to let me get to know the people who report to you. Every company has some sort of process where people have regular meeting times with their team members, weekly or monthly, or whatever the expected timeframe might be. During those times, a good leader should expect team managers to bring in people who work for them to give updates on the projects they're working on. These people deserve the opportunity to demonstrate how they go about solving problems and what their methods look like. Their potential can only be assessed by leadership if they are given the chance to communicate directly with leadership.

I know this concept sounds very simple, and my solution might sound a bit harsh, but your people must understand that you are not interested in wasting their time, so that they assume what you ask for is necessary, one hundred percent of the time.

I almost always have a good handle on what my direct reports' skills look like, but I want to see how some other people are doing, how they're developing, how they're growing. I can also see what they need to work on. By doing that, I can provide input to their manager on changes they could make to improve themselves. It might be their communication style, their attention to detail, or their presentation skills. It could be any number of things, but I'm not going to know about it and can't develop an opinion about how to help them if I never see them in action.

On my teams, we usually meet once a month as a group. We have an agenda that we run through. I expect to see those lower level people present what they're working on at these meetings. I think it's great visibility, it's great training, and it's a great opportunity to grow.

Expectation: I expect one hundred percent responsiveness one hundred percent of the time. I am not a leader who spends his time managing everyone else's projects. I'm not the leader, for example, who will take your expense report and add it up to make sure you did the math right. I'm not the kind of leader who gives you a list of tasks to perform, and then ticks them off as they get completed. I expect you to keep track of all that on your own, but one hundred percent of the time, I expect you to do what you said you were going to do, on time.

I might have some specifics that I need you to follow up on or find some information related to an assignment I know you're working on, but I will always try to give you time to find the answer. I might say, "If you have two weeks to work out what I'm asking you, do you think you can have those answers for me by then?"

If that person says "yes," then two weeks later, when we have our scheduled time together, he/she can be certain that my list of questions will include, "Where are we on that? What information do you have for me at this point?" This kind of interaction differs from the sort of micromanaging I will not do because I expect my people to have the competence and initiative to manage their own day-to-day tasks.

I was shocked in my first managerial position in the late eighties when I was asked to move to Atlanta, Georgia to run a special markets sales division. I had people reporting to me from Atlanta, Baltimore,

Washington, Richmond, the Carolinas, Alabama, Louisiana, Miami, and Orlando. It was an entry-level manager position, but I had twenty-three direct reports covering a wide geographical area. What shocked me during the first month was how few of my people handed in the reports I requested. I thought I had become pretty good at follow-through early in my career. If your boss asks you to do something, you do it, right? Their lack of compliance was a real surprise. If I said, "I need this report on Friday afternoon," some people did it, some handed it in late, and some never did it at all.

After the first thirty days, I started meeting with people and asking, "Why aren't you doing this for me?"

They usually said something like, "Oh, I didn't realize that it was important to you."

I was so surprised that they thought I would ask them to spend their time doing something I didn't think was necessary, and I remember looking each of them in the eye and saying, "So, if you're not doing what I ask you to do, how do I know you're doing what your customers ask you to do? I pay you. They pay us. If you're not doing what I want you to do, and I can't be confident that you're doing what your customers want you to do, then we need to have a conversation about that."

Over the next thirty days, I figured out who was interested in complying with my direction as their new boss and who was not, and therefore, who going to be staying on my team long-term and who was not. I know this concept sounds very simple, and my solution might sound a bit harsh, but your people must understand that you are not interested in wasting their time, so that they assume what you ask for *is* necessary, one hundred percent of the time. If you do this, your people will comply, your information flow will be smooth and fast, and your business will move along toward its goals as quickly as possible.

Similarly, I expect my team to respond when I ask a question, request a meeting, or even just reach out to see how they're doing. People's lack of responsiveness constantly appalls me, and I find it rather ironic. We have multiple modes of communication literally at our fingertips, but I frequently find that people are not timely in their responses or that they do not reply at all.

It is a matter of integrity, and at the end of the day, I want to know that the people who work for me and with me are people of integrity. It's just that simple.

This is unacceptable and can be problematic for many reasons, but think about it from a purely pragmatic standpoint. If you are the person waiting on a reply, and you don't receive one, you probably start to create a story in your mind about why that person hasn't responded, and those stories are rarely positive. It is our natural human tendency to think, "Is it me? Have I done something wrong? Am I not important enough to garner a reply?" Our minds go to places like that rather than assuming the best-case scenario. Obviously, this creates undue tension and stress not just in business, but in life as well. Respond—it reflects well on you and makes others feel valued.

Expectation: Confidential information must be kept confidential. This is, without a doubt, my most important expectation. As you take on more responsibilities as a leader, you will deal with profit margins, customer contracts, sensitive HR issues about people who are underperforming or have not yet made public that they plan to move on, and so forth. As a leader, you will have to share some of that information with members of your team, and you will be privy to information from leaders of other divisions who need to bring you into the loop on issues that will ultimately affect your business as well. That sort of information must be kept confidential one hundred percent of the time. I tell all my teams early on, "If I find out that you cannot keep confidential information confidential, you will not work for me. I have zero tolerance. We'll simply walk over to another department and try to find you something else to do."

Some people might say that is too direct or even that I'm being a bully, but I'm not trying to be unfairly harsh. I'm just being clear about how I feel, how extremely important this is to me, and it's only important to me because it's important to the business. I've shared information with you because it's necessary that I do so, but sometimes that information cannot be shared with others, and so you get to make a choice. If you choose not to follow my instructions to keep certain information confidential, which would be considered standard practice in any company, then you're putting your career at risk and may be jeopardizing other people's careers or the success of the business. It is a matter of integrity, and at the end of the day, I want to know that the people who work for me and with me are people of integrity. It's just that simple.

It's important to realize that if you have developed an environment of trust in your organization, you can have direct, confidential conversations with your people, and they can be entirely honest with you because they know you will be able to help them move forward without fear of public repercussions. Without this sense of trust, factions inevitably form and alliances are brokered that can stand in the way of your business achieving results.

Someone once told me, "Be strict with your strategy but compassionate with your people." This is excellent advice. When your people know that you are being direct with them out of respect for them and to keep the work process moving forward, when they already realize that you value them as people, then they don't take professional criticism personally, and everyone can move forward.

For Reflection

What are your top four to five expectations of others in the workplace? Write them down along with an explanation of the importance of each.

Chapter 7

Determine and Articulate Your Work Style

Once I've informed my team members about what I expect them to do and not do, it's important to put these preferences into a context that will make sense for them. I accomplish this by explaining my work style. Giving them as much insight as possible into my professional self will provide the necessary context to help them understand how we can best work together.

An important aspect of my work style that I want my team to understand is that I am an introvert. I believe in the Myers Briggs® Personality Typing System, that people have dominant elements of their personalities that drive how they become energized and help to identify how they prefer to work. According to this assessment, I am an ISTJ – heavy on the "I," meaning I am an unmistakable introvert. As I have become a more mature leader, I have become even more of an introvert. Interacting with other people for long periods of time drains me of energy, and I need time by myself to recharge. I use my time alone to think, to process information that's been given to me, and to make decisions about how to best move forward.

On the opposite end of the spectrum are obviously the extroverts, those who are energized in the presence of and interaction with others.

Of course, extroverts still need some time alone to process what they're learning day-to-day, and even though I am an introvert, I still enjoy interacting with others and debates that challenge my ways of thinking. I've come to realize, however, that this kind of interaction exhausts me, so when I feel like I have all the information I need from a given conversation, I'm not interested in any more debate.

I explain this to my teams, that there will be days when I have my office door shut. If it's shut, it's because I'm working, and during those times, I prefer they don't call me, knock on my door, or ask my secretary to see if I'm available. I don't ask to be alone for more than maybe an hour or so at a time, often less, and I try to do it during times when most of the team is not in the office, maybe early in the morning, late in the afternoon, or over lunch. I try not to take time that would be beneficial for them to stop by my office and certainly not during our scheduled meeting times. When the door is shut, though, I am working, and I make it clear to my team that this time working alone is very important to me.

There are times, as an introvert, that I need to get away entirely. For example, if we're traveling for business, I rarely do anything with my team after dinner. Half the time, I don't even do dinner with my team, but one hundred percent of the time, I don't do anything with the team after dinner. I've gotten all the input I need, I've had all the social stimulus I need. I go back to my room to do what I need to do—answer emails, call home, relax, whatever.

Everybody has a story about a manager who joined the team at a bar, or wherever they ended up going to socialize together after dinner, and something bad happened.

I've worked with new teams when we've had to travel together before I had the chance to explain this about myself. If I skipped dinner with the team or did not join them out after dinner, some of these new team members wondered, "Maybe he's mad at us," or "Maybe he doesn't like us." As soon as I got the opportunity to tell them about my leadership style and my desire to spend my evenings alone, they understood. It all goes back to clear communication.

Needing my evening time alone falls right in line with something I believe very strongly—nothing good happens for a leader after dinner. It doesn't matter how late in the evening it is. Sometimes after a long day on the road, dinner may not wrap up until nine-thirty or ten at night, but nothing good happens for a leader after that point in the day. Everybody has a story about a manager who joined the team at a bar, or wherever they ended up going to socialize together after dinner, and something bad happened.

I'm not just talking about the possibility of overindulging or misbehaving. More often, the leaders simply open themselves up to other people's social perceptions. "He talked to this other person more than he talked to me," or "She spoke badly about that project from a few years ago, and I was involved in that," or "He doesn't seem to respect that person who is a friend of mine." Nothing good happens for a leader after dinner.

This is a hard lesson to learn. Going out with the team is fun. It makes you "popular," so to speak, but it can also cause major divisions in your team. In one assignment, when I met with my team members one on one during the first thirty days, I heard an earful about the former boss who went to happy hour every Friday with part of the team. The problem there is the word "part." Apparently, it was an open invitation, everyone was invited, but for various reasons, some people could not attend. They had commitments at home they had to attend to, so over time, tensions grew within the team because it appeared that the boss treated the happy hour group differently. They were labeled "favorites," and the rest of the team felt upset and excluded.

I will admit, I learned this lesson the hard way, myself. Years ago, when I was a less experienced leader, there were a couple of times when I did join the team out after dinner. Maybe I had a couple drinks. Maybe I said some things I wish I hadn't said, and believe me, the tension that created got back to me and did some serious damage to the team. I used to leave a voicemail for the entire team every Friday night recapping the week and calling attention to specific successes and areas of improvement for the week ahead. One Friday evening, I was out with some of the team, and someone suggested that I pass the phone around and let everyone say a word or two on the weekly voicemail. Like a fool, I did it, and on Monday morning, I sure did regret it.

I thought to myself, "I'll fix that. I'll change my behavior. I won't go out with my team after dinner ever again." I made a decisive, but simple adaptation to my leadership style based on a specific experience that has made a significant improvement in my ability to lead a team smoothly forward.

Another element of my work style is my belief that vacations are vacations. Don't call me. I won't call you. I know there are always exceptions to this, and as a leader, you must respond to urgent matters that come up unexpectedly, especially if it has something to do with a customer. What I'm referring to here are situations that could be filed under "business as usual." Leaders need vacations just like ev-

What I'm essentially communicating to my team members when I tell them not to contact me is that I know I've put together a strong group of people, and that within the timeframe of one week, I believe they are capable enough to resolve any sort of "business as usual" problem that might arise in my absence.

erybody else. You need to be able to unplug. You need to be able to get away. When I tell people I'm going on vacation, I say, "I might check my email. I might not."

It's hard not to check in while I'm away, but if I end up working while I'm on vacation, then I'm not really on vacation at all. I'm just working from someplace nice. What I'm essentially communicating to my team members when I tell them not to contact me is that I know I've put together a strong group of people, and that within the timeframe of one week, I believe they are capable enough to resolve any sort of "business as usual" problem that might arise in my absence.

My team members know how I work, and so they have a good idea about how I would address some, if not most, issues. I know my team members are qualified to answer day-to-day questions without having to hear from me directly, and I need my people to have the courage and confidence to make those kinds of decisions when I'm not reachable.

Years ago, when I had been with the company only seven or eight years, I had a manager who had no leadership principles at all. He was random, unpredictable, and quite aggressive. In fact, he was a bit of a bully, and when I reported to him, I had a very difficult assignment involving long hours and considerable follow-up. It was a real grind, and I really needed a vacation, so I seized on the first opportunity I could to get away and headed to northern Arkansas with my family. I was out enjoying myself on the lake, having a great time. Long before the advent of the cell phone, I was completely unreachable, or so I thought.

Several days in, my manager, after unsuccessfully attempting to find me, actually called my in-laws. Assuming it must be an emergency, my in-laws drove two hours down to the lake and my father-in-law got in a boat and rode out onto the water to find us. "You need to call your boss," he hollered at me across the water. "It's urgent. You need to call him right now."

I had no idea what could have possibly gone so wrong. I thought somebody died or maybe there had been a major leadership change. Maybe I was fired. I didn't know what on earth had happened, but I was worried, so I raced the boat back to the little house where we were staying. Because it didn't have a phone (and there was certainly no email back then), I got in the car and drove down the road to a small grocery store that had a payphone outside. I called my boss, who wasn't at his desk, so I left a message for him to call the number of the pay phone at this country store. Then I stood there and waited for him to call back.

After almost two hours, the phone finally rang. I answered frantically, "What's going on?"

Calmly, he answered, "I finally got a chance to read your script for the sales meeting presentation that's coming up in a couple of weeks, and I've got a few things we need to talk about."

"What?"

"Yeah, I have a few of things we need to talk about on this script."

This was maybe a Thursday. I would be back in the office the following Monday, and the sales meeting was still a couple of weeks away.

"*Really?*" I asked. "That's what you wanted to talk to me about?" I couldn't believe it. It had worried my in-laws and inconvenienced them terribly. It had disrupted the day on the lake I was having with my family, and I was so mad that it ruined the rest of my vacation time. In fact, when I got back to the office, I was still mad. That experience really stuck with me and I've made sure to never do that to other people.

Everyone needs time away from the office, away from the stresses of day-to-day work life. Everyone needs time to reconnect with family and friends. Respecting someone's vacation time is like respecting their privacy. They deserve it, and so do you. If you are a strong leader, then you have a team in place who can handle the normal complications that arise in your business because you have given them clear communication over time about how you prefer these sorts of situations to be handled. You will be back on Monday.

If you adopt this method of communicating your nits, expectations, and work style to your team, I suggest you walk your team through the rest of your leadership philosophy first, which I detail in the following chapters. Then, talk about your work style and your expectations, followed by your nits, last. I have communicated with new teams several different ways and found that saving the nits for last makes them less jarring for a new team to hear than as the very first information you give them about yourself. Give them some insight into your personality first, and they will have some context around your preferences that will make more sense.

For Reflection

How would you describe your work style? What do you need in order to be successful on a daily basis? If you have never completed a Myers Briggs assessment, or something similar, you should do so.

Chapter 8

Listen Carefully and Ask Good Questions

When I was a salesperson in Arlington, Texas in 1984, my boss's boss, the regional VP of sales, left me a voicemail early in the week that he would be calling me on Saturday morning. Actually, his secretary left me the message, and for the rest of that week, I was petrified that I had done something wrong. He was an intimidating, imposing kind of guy, and it was Saturday for crying out loud—naturally, I assumed there must be a problem. As it turned out, he just called to tell me what a great job I was doing and to ask me how things were going. That was it, and for the next hour and a half, he listened to everything I had to say. He didn't interrupt me or rush me along. He *really* listened and asked questions to help clarify as I rambled on. As our conversation concluded, he thanked *me* for *my* time. I'll never forget that. It made me feel special and valued, just to be listened to. It was a simple gesture, but it made a lasting impression. Listening and asking questions are paramount to being a good leader, but listening is one of the most underdeveloped and underleveraged skills in most leaders I have encountered.

I remember a certain corporate guest speaker at a regional sales meeting during my first year as a salesperson named Clark Randall. He oversaw all our product development, and I was impressed with him and intrigued by the process of making product.

In his presentation, Clark talked extensively about listening. He stressed the importance of asking questions and really listening to people's responses, hearing their opinions, and understanding their emotions. He elaborated on ways to act on what you heard. He referenced a book titled, *How to Speak and How to Listen*, by Mortimer J. Adler. I bought it immediately, and that book, along with Mr. Randall's talk, changed everything. From that point forward, I thought differently about the way I communicated with not only customers, but everyone, including friends and family.

Listening and asking questions are paramount to being a good leader, but listening is one of the most underdeveloped and underleveraged skills in most leaders I have encountered.

People who listen and ask great questions grow faster and go further in an organization than people who do all the talking. I am certain that people who do all the talking aren't learning very much because they don't take the time to let anyone else give them new information.

I've certainly been guilty of this at times myself. Homer Evans, one of my early mentors, taught me a valuable lesson about listening. If you read the introduction to this book, you already know that I think quite highly of Homer. He was a corporate vice president when I worked for him in my first corporate assignment in a junior product development role.

Usually, when people report to a corporate VP, they prepare thoroughly, so when it comes time to present progress, they are armed and ready to answer any number of questions the VP might pose. Homer rarely ever said anything while information was being presented to him during a meeting. In a one-hour meeting, he might not talk for the first thirty minutes. He might ask some clarifying questions along the way, but sometimes he would wait until even the last fifteen minutes or so, and then he would ask two or three questions to the group, and those few questions would unlock the problem we were trying to solve.

"You are the master of what you don't say and the slave to what you do. Choose wisely."

He was excellent at listening and asking questions. I never remember him talking for more than a few minutes at a time in *any* meeting because he already knew what he knew. He wanted to know what everyone else knew. He listened until he had the information he was looking for, and then he would be able to pinpoint the areas that needed the most attention. He was specific about what he wanted done, who he wanted to do it, and exactly when he wanted it completed. Everyone would leave the meeting feeling confident in his decisions, knowing exactly what they were going to do, by when, and what was expected of everyone else.

I had worked for Homer about three months when he came by my cubicle early one morning. "Wayne," he asked, "do you have a three-by-five?"

Back then, that's how we kept track of things. Before iPads and smart phones, we wrote on three-by-five note cards and kept them in our pockets. Of course, I had a tall stack of three-by-fives on my desk, so I grabbed one quickly to hand to him, but instead, he said, "Find a pen and write this down, young man." After a brief pause, he continued, "You are the master of what you don't say and the slave to what you do. Choose wisely."

Then, he walked away.

Naturally, I started freaking out, thinking wildly about what I must have said to make Homer feel I could benefit from that advice.

Obviously, somewhere along the way, I had broken the golden rule of talking when I should have been listening, and he gave me a strong, clear, pointed developmental message. Although I spent the next several days in panic mode worrying that I had ruined my career by talking too much, it forever made an impact on me. Talk less, listen more, and ask good questions.

In 2002, I was placed in charge of a corporate initiative to target some new competencies we needed to develop as an enterprise. I was partnered with a corporate VP who had some experience working with outside consultants, and the two of us were asked to bring in a handful of consultants and make a decision about who we should hire to help us develop these competencies.

We asked four or five consulting agencies to come in. The first group came in with five or six senior people decked out in their finest suits and ties, who showed us beautifully produced slides and videos and testimonials about their work. It was all very impressive. Another group came through with a couple senior people and a room full of the best and brightest MBA graduates from the top schools.

Another highly recommended consulting firm called The Partnering Group, better known as TPG, came in with the president and one of the partners leading the pitch. They weren't dressed very formally; they looked like the people I worked with every day. The first page of the presentation showed a timeline of how they would proceed with the work we were asking them to do for us, and the second page was titled, "Here's what we're going to do today."

One of our corporate VP's stopped the presentation and said, "I really don't want to see any slides. I just want you to talk to me. Tell me what you do."

The president of TPG at the time, a man by the name of John Dye, who later became a great friend of mine, shut down the presentation laptop. They didn't have overheads. They didn't have handouts. John asked, "What do you want to know?"

For the next hour and a half, we talked about what we were trying to accomplish. John asked us questions and provided us many examples. He'd hear one of us make a comment and he'd say, "Expand on that. What do you mean by that? Where in your organization are you having these problems?"

One of the young men on John's team had probably spent two weeks putting together a slick, eighty-page presentation. It was well done with numerous, cool production details. It was likely all he had worked on for quite a while, and many times during our conversation, he wanted so badly to open that laptop. He'd say, "Hey, I can show you a slide. I can give you an example of exactly what we're talking about."

Every time, John replied, "No. They don't want to see any slides, so we're not going to show them any."

His tremendous wisdom and experience led him to listen and do exactly what we wanted, and at the end of those two hours, John gave us a proposal, and a few weeks later, we signed a very lucrative consulting agreement with his company. They actually ended up working with us for years after that on all sorts of projects. It was impressive to see a man at that level completely shut down their presentation and just ask us, "What do you want to know?" It was a beautiful example of listening and asking questions, one of the best examples I've seen, and he earned his company that contract.

Another great listener who asks great questions is my wife, Aviva. She has worked for a couple different consulting firms, spent fifteen years in corporate life, and now owns her own consulting firm. Her core foundational skill is her ability to listen and ask great questions. It's an amazing thing to see how she does this over and over again, both when she was working in a large corporation and now as a consultant.

During a typical project, she will spend the first thirty to sixty days doing extensive fact finding, trying to lay a foundation of information about what a company is currently doing. I bet I've heard her ask clients these questions hundreds of times: "Can you explain how you do that? Tell me about your top three strategies. How do you measure them? How do you train your people? How do you communicate to your organization?"

It's the listening skills and the questions you ask that will penetrate issues and lead to positive results.

Aviva attended Rice University and Northwestern University, and she's as smart as anyone I've ever met, so she clearly has the academic and technical training to put together a very articulate, well thought out, impressive presentation. It is her listening and questioning skills, however, that built the foundation for her success.

If you listen and ask questions, you'll gather information that you can then translate into a proposal, solution, or course of action. It's the listening skills and the questions you ask that will penetrate issues and lead to positive results.

Listening and asking questions can also help you to master the timing of your communication, which is key to getting your message across and motivating your team to deliver. If you communicate too soon, people won't have the right context, and your message may come across as unnecessarily alarming. If you communicate too late, you lose impact, or you may appear as though you did not gather timely information. If you communicate too frequently, your most important messages will get lost among all the others and they will fail to gain traction. Listening more and talking less will ultimately allow you to craft powerful messages that will be heard.

For Reflection

Who do you consider to be a great listener? What qualities make that person a skillful listener? Do you perceive yourself to be a good listener? What circumstances make it difficult for you to be the kind of listener you need to be? Can you think of a time when not listening caused you to fail? Can you think of a time when listening well caused you to succeed?

Chapter 9

Double-Edged Sword

Communication is obviously important, and as a leader, it can be a powerful tool to propel your team to great success, or it can be a destructive weapon that leads to your team's ultimate failure. Knowing how and when to communicate effectively is integral to any leadership philosophy.

Leaders communicate with their teams for many reasons: to inform, to motivate, to redirect, to clarify, and to reinforce. It is important for a leader to be disciplined in that communication. People are overloaded today with information and messaging. If I do not have a clearly defined objective in mind before I present something to my team, there is a good chance it's going to get lost in the milieu of all the other communications they receive that day.

In addition to being clear about what I am trying to communicate, I must also be careful not to overcommunicate. This is part of the delicate balance that leaders must achieve. When I think back even twenty years ago, I would've given anything to have the capability at my fingertips to send a quick text message from out in the field right at the moment I needed to convey something of importance. As it was, I had to wait until I got back to the office to type up an email. Often, by that point, the urgency of my message had waned, or I had to wait on a reply which might not come immediately. To think, email seemed like the answer to all our troubles twenty years ago. Don't even get me started talking about work before computers!

My point is that as technology evolves, we have increasing access to broader and more expedient means of communication. This can be a very good thing, but it can also be abused. Leaders need to be considerate of their team's time outside of work and must fight the urge to hit "send" every time a new idea crystalizes. I have worked for leaders whose mentality was, "I think; therefore, I must speak," or text, or whatever it might be. A good leader knows that too much communication overburdens people and is perceived as micromanaging. More importantly, it lessens the significance of the message. Convey only what needs to be conveyed—people will pay more attention that way and will realize that you mean what you say.

People are overloaded today with information and messaging. If I do not have a clearly defined objective in mind before I present something to my team, there is a good chance it's going to get lost in the milieu of all the other communications they receive that day.

Technology has presented another obstacle when it comes to communication. Everyone typically attends meetings with some sort of electronic device for note-taking, whether it be a laptop, tablet, phone, or whatever the latest and greatest happens to be. The good thing about this is that it allows us to quickly access information and research topics during meetings that we used to have to put off until we returned to our desks. In many ways, it speeds up meetings and makes for a more efficient workflow.

However, more frequently, my experience is that it can cause problems during meetings, and I bet you've seen and experienced this same reality. You're in a meeting having a discussion and something comes up that needs clarification, so one or two (or more) people immediately drop their heads, zone in on their screens, and slip into research mode. This, in and of itself, is not a negative. The problem occurs when they're busy looking something up while the meeting and discussions continue. They end up missing what's happening in the here and now because they're too busy trying to find some tidbit of information that probably could've waited until later anyway.

> *There must still be some value to personal interaction. We must shut down our devices and deal with each other in person, at least some of the time.*

I know there are people who say they can multi-task, who say that just because they're looking something up doesn't mean they're not listening. I would like to believe that, but experience tells me it's simply not true.

As leaders, we must become more thoughtful about how and when we communicate. If we are all going to sit in a room on our individual devices, then perhaps we didn't need a face to face meeting in the first place, and I suspect that sometimes, that is indeed the case. The business at hand *could* be handled via email, but I do not think that is the case all the time. There must still be some value to personal interaction. We must shut down our devices and deal with each other in person, at least some of the time.

When I am in a meeting, I need my team to be fully present and fully engaged in the moment, even if that means setting aside the laptops and tablets. This is not an easy ask and not always a popular stance, but it is important to me. That is really the point—if you are the leader, it is up to you to communicate to your team in a straightforward and unapologetic manner what you need and expect.

I realize that it isn't always feasible or productive to "outlaw" all screens during an entire meeting, so as the leader, I have to figure out how to balance my needs with what is required to get work done. Perhaps it is as simple as structuring the meeting time in such a way that affords for both dedicated discussion time as well as time for research. Again, that's the delicate balance I must strive to create, and if I am the leader of my team, then that's my job.

For Reflection

Would you say you have the tendency to overcommunicate or under communicate? What is your preferred mode of communication to your team? Do you think the advent of newer technologies has made communication easier or more difficult? What are the positive and negative impacts you see on your teams and in your business?

Courage

Leadership requires courage—it is not for the faint of heart. On an almost daily basis, it becomes necessary to summon courage that you didn't even know you possessed. It is not easy to take an unpopular stance when others disagree. It is not easy to keep confidentiality when all you want to do is gossip or vent. It is not easy to give credit to your team for positive results but hold yourself accountable when the team misses the mark. It is not easy to speak the truth when others do not want to hear it or to know when to keep silent when others are prodding you to say things you know you shouldn't. Leadership is hard work, and if you're going to be successful, you must learn to take risks and lead courageously.

CHAPTER 10

Cultivate Courage Over Time

ACHIEVING A LEADERSHIP POSITION does not guarantee you possess courage. Leadership and courage are two very different things. Leadership requires it, but you don't automatically acquire it. Unfortunately, you don't walk into your office on your first day as a leader and find a sign on your wall that says, "Congratulations! You have courage! Here's a three-step handbook on how to demonstrate your new-found courage."

Courage is cultivated over time by having a set of principles you operate from, even during the tough times. Courage is about making difficult decisions, about knowing the metrics you need to hit and believing that the team can rely on you to make the critical decisions at the critical times that will get them there.

I've seen incredibly strong managers promoted to higher leadership positions, but when they get there, they don't know what to do, and so they do very little. In my experience, managers are the backbone of any organization. If you give good managers ten tasks to do, and you give them direction, they will execute those ten tasks exceptionally well. They get focused, they hit their budget, they manage every metric down to the third decimal point. They prove themselves to be strong managers. As managers, they can lead a team to achieve a challenging goal when given specific direction, but as leaders, they sometimes find that they don't have the courage necessary to provide that direction, to take that risk, to make those decisions. They become almost paralyzed by fear. They are so afraid of doing the wrong thing, that instead, they do nothing. Solid, reliable, and predictable leadership requires courage—you must overcome the fear of being wrong. Otherwise, you'll be stagnant, and success in business never results from standing still.

You must have a solid foundation of principles along with courage to keep yourself from being reckless. Recklessness all but guarantees failure.

I've seen the opposite happen as well. I've seen some incredibly strong managers promoted to leadership positions, and suddenly, they make very reckless choices. They take their success at the lower levels of leadership as a basis for confidence, but neglect to remember that they were provided with proper direction by their leaders at that time. I believe these sorts of individuals fail because their decisions are not founded on a set of guiding principles they have established for themselves. These may include financial principles or metrics, personality traits they should bring to the job every day, or any philosophy they come to value. You must have a solid foundation of principles along with courage to keep yourself from being reckless. Recklessness all but guarantees failure.

Sometimes, leaders, particularly new leaders, take charge of a division and make some very bold claims about what they can do over a short period of time. They appear exceedingly confident, but often, over time, those leaders lose credibility, and their character takes a punch. If their bold decision-making is not based on measured choices using sound facts and the experience to know how to interpret those facts, those decisions are reckless, and goals fail to be achieved.

When a leader is too timid or too bold, it's a sign that he or she is operating at a level that is above his or her capabilities. They may look courageous, they may feel like they're being courageous, but they're not. Leaders who are truly courageous can accomplish what it is they say they are going to accomplish. They have already demonstrated over time that they're going to take measured risks against sound assumptions and solid information, and they're going to lead their team to success in a measured, predictable way that everyone is going to be proud of.

FOR REFLECTION

What does "courage" look like to you? Has there been a time in your professional life when you acted courageously? Has there been a time when fear got the better of you? What are you most afraid of in your career?

Chapter 11

Make Decisions and Manage Tension

The decisions that leaders make in the workplace should not be driven by random assumptions, opinions, or any of the other intangible factors that are always present in the workplace. Instead, decisions should always be based on a leader's current business strategy. The best leaders internalize and integrate their business strategy into every single one of their plans and actions. All work must be done against a strategy which, in turn, must be aligned with a profit and loss statement.

I've used this phrase with my team for a very long time: "Facts are our friends." Give me the facts, and only the facts, and we'll go from there. It's been my experience that if you have the facts, and you share those facts with the people you work with, you will all make the same decisions the vast majority of the time. It's when you don't have the facts, when you talk about assumptions and opinions, that you get distracted, you become dysfunctional, and you end up wasting time and resources. If you start with the facts, and you have a solid strategy that you can articulate

Successful leaders seek out and encourage debate on big issues. Diversity of thought and debate are crucial.

and measure against those facts, and hold them up to your profit and loss statement, you will be successful.

Decision-making can and will lead to tension because not everyone on your team will agree with the decisions you make one hundred percent of the time. A leader cannot be afraid of this. Leaders must manage the tension created in their organization when they make decisions, and the most important way to do this is to listen to your people and make sure they feel as if they've been heard. I always tell my team that "support" and "agreement" are not necessarily the same thing. You can support my decisions even if you don't agree, and likewise, I can support yours even when I disagree.

Manage the tension, but remember that a certain amount of tension is a good thing.

When someone on my team disagrees with my decisions, I invite him/her in for a conversation. I listen to the opposing point of view and assure my team member that I understand where he/she is coming from. I ask for support despite our differing stances, and almost always, that individual walks out of my office feeling validated and willing to commit to my plan of action. Leaders must be courageous enough to allow for disagreement and to have difficult conversations about those disagreements.

Successful leaders seek out and encourage debate on big issues. Diversity of thought and debate are crucial. You've gathered and trained a world-class team. You've earned their trust, which enables them to feel empowered to speak their minds. It is then your responsibility as the leader to listen to the team, gather the facts, and make the decision. Let the team know when the debate is over, and then assign tasks that are crystal clear. Define the goal, outline the steps the team must take to get there, give your people dates, metrics, and let everyone on that project know what everyone else is doing.

When you end the debate and make the decision, you will almost inevitably create tension. If this tension goes unmanaged, it can build up and cause hesitation among team members or even cause someone to fly out of formation and take an action that does not quite align with your direction. This wastes valuable time.

Manage the tension, but remember that a certain amount of tension is a good thing. Too little tension could mean that your team doesn't trust you enough to speak their minds. If this is the case, you may not get all the facts you need to make the best possible decision. If everyone's head is nodding throughout an entire discussion, that can be a bad sign. If there is tension, then people's perceptions and opinions are being challenged, even yours, and that's good. This can be hard to achieve unless you have your finger on the pulse of your team and the pressing issues, but if you've built the necessary level of trust through predictable leadership, thoughtful debate will ensue, and the best decision can be made.

For Reflection

Do you consider yourself to be a decisive leader? Why or why not? What makes it difficult for you to be decisive? How do you currently handle tension on your team?

Chapter 12

Hold Yourself Accountable and Give Your Team Credit

Leadership requires accountability. I believe this is the single most important aspect of being a good leader. As the leader of an organization, you're going to be held accountable to very specific measures. Those measures might be based on a new product you're going to develop, the speed of delivery, or reducing the cost of shipments. There might be many aspects of the business that the organization is looking to you to oversee. It is your job to know the facts, to have a set of metrics to guide you, to make the decisions, and to hold yourself accountable for the results.

A good leader knows that he/she does not work in a vacuum. Goals are reached because of teams of dedicated people pulling together to get the job done. It's never a one man or woman operation, or at least, it shouldn't be. When something goes incredibly well, the first thing out of your mouth, as the leader, should be, "Thank you," followed by, "Let me tell you a little bit about this individual, or team, and what they did to help us get this over the goal line." If somebody in finance or marketing who doesn't report up through your organization deserves some recognition, take the time to credit them as well. A good leader has the courage to give credit where credit is due, rather than hog the limelight all to himself.

The flip side of that coin is that if you have a bad quarter or a bad year, if the train comes off the rails, if a project ends in negative results, and you get called out on the carpet to address it, the first words out of your mouth should be, "I'm responsible. I'm accountable for this mess."

When that happens, and it *will* happen, be ready with a specific plan. Be courageous enough to say, "These are the actions I'm going to take today to start getting things back on track. These are the four or five things I'm going to do over time. Here are the dates when I expect them to be done. Here's how much they're going to cost, and here's the outcome I expect by this point in time."

Don't make excuses. Don't say things like, "The product didn't sell," or "The marketing wasn't very good," or "The supply chain was sloppy." None of that, because if any of it is true, everyone probably already knows it anyway. As a leader, you need to step up and say, "I'm accountable. I own it. I'm responsible. These are the things I'm going to do ASAP to fix it. I'd like to meet with you in a week. I'd like to meet with you in a month," whatever timeframe you feel is appropriate.

> *Crediting your team for achieving positive results and accepting responsibility when goals are not met will earn you much credibility with your team.*

Many times, leaders fall into the trap of spending their time talking about what *other* people should be doing to help them get their job done. It sounds something like, "I saw our commercial last night, and it just wasn't effective enough. It should have done this..." or "I looked over the new product offering and if we could just lower the cost we could sell so much more." It can even be blatant excuses like, "The reason this other team is looking better than ours is because they benefitted from the great results our team achieved" or "We don't have the right people."

The list goes on and on, but if you become that kind of leader, people will start to label you a "whiner" or a "complainer." It will be evident to everyone that you are not accountable, and before you know it, you're not a leader anymore, or maybe you're even looking for another job. If you're the leader, the buck really does stop at you.

The key takeaway here is this—stand up and be accountable. Crediting your team for achieving positive results and accepting responsibility when goals are not met will earn you much credibility with your team. I believe it should be a part of every leader's philosophy, without a doubt. This might be a tough concept to accept, and it took me a long time to accept it as a positive aspect of professional behavior, but I guarantee it will pay off.

For Reflection

Describe a time when you received credit for an accomplishment from your boss. Have you ever been robbed of credit you deserved? Do you give credit to others when it is due? Describe a time when you accepted responsibility for a mistake or failure. What makes that difficult to do? Do you need to be better at giving credit or accepting responsibility?

CHAPTER 13

KEEP YOUR MOUTH SHUT

WE ALL GET FRUSTRATED and need to vent sometimes, but as a leader, that is a luxury you cannot afford. Hopefully, you have someone in your life outside of your workplace who can listen to you blow off steam and support you, but it is imperative to keep your mouth shut at the office, especially when it comes to giving feedback about your boss to other people. It's not worth the risk. I have learned through experience that when you share feedback about your boss with someone else, it almost always gets played back in a different context than what you intended. Only give feedback about your boss if your boss asks you for it directly. In that situation, your boss trusts you and you owe him or her your honest and thorough opinion, but avoid it when someone else approaches you.

I'm sure you've been in situations where someone has said, "Hey, I'm collecting some feedback on your boss. It's just standard procedure, and I'll be sure to keep your answers just between us." Or you're having lunch with someone and they'll say, "Tell me about your boss." Whenever this happens, you should essentially say your boss is great. He or she is a great leader. You are on the same page. Do not fall into the trap of criticizing your boss to other people. If your boss hears pieces of your comments out of context, or someone with an agenda gets ahold of some information that can be credited to you, it can lead to irreparable damage to your relationship with your boss.

I speak from experience. This happened to me once, where my comments were played back to my boss in sound bites by someone who had a very clear prerogative. A sound bite, in this case, meant that someone took a piece of what I said and added it to other pieces of what other people said for the purpose of spinning the narrative she wanted to tell. An example might sound something like this. You say, "My boss is a great leader, he is a great communicator, he has a vision for the future, he meets regularly with my team, but I wish he would spend more time in the marketplace."

In my experience, if someone is wanting to tell a negative story about your boss, your input might get replayed this way, "We've collected information that you don't spend time in the marketplace. We have an issue."

Like I said, I've made this mistake before. It was a lesson I'll never forget. We had a consulting firm in, talking to key stakeholders, asking questions, and collecting feedback—fairly run of the mill procedure. During one of those conversations, I was asked several questions about my boss, such as, "What do you like about him?" and "What do you wish he would do differently?" Now, my boss and I were friends, long-time friends, but when asked to give feedback about him, I was honest and direct. Nothing I said was untrue. Despite the promise of total anonymity, my comments got

Do not fall into the trap of criticizing your boss to other people. If your boss hears pieces of your comments out of context, or someone with an agenda gets ahold of some information that can be credited to you, it can lead to irreparable damage to your relationship with your boss.

played back in numerous, out of context "sound bites" that twisted my words around, and as you can imagine, it did not go over well. In the end, as the situation escalated, it destroyed not only the friendship we had, but the professional relationship as well. We never recovered, and for a long time, work was absolutely miserable for me.

From that point forward, I've made the conscious choice to stay in formation and not provide feedback, even when I thought there might be areas where my boss could improve. You might think you're helping your team by suggesting areas your leader could improve. You might even just feel relief in voicing some frustrations, but it's been my experience that staying in formation has always worked better by comparison. It takes courage to stay in formation, to keep quiet when you want to speak up, to put your head down and plow ahead, but it is almost always the right choice to make.

This is a simple concept and one that is easy to control because all you have to do is make a choice. Don't give feedback about your boss unless your boss asks for it, and then you can give your honest feedback directly to him or her.

For Reflection

Have you had an experience where you spoke about your boss when you shouldn't have? Have you had an experience where you chose to keep your thoughts and feelings about your boss to yourself? What happened in each scenario? What did you learn from those experiences?

Chapter 14

Achieve Balance

Great leaders have balance in their lives. They balance the things that make them whole, whether it's work, family, hobbies, health, faith, or personal growth, whatever it is for them as individuals. They identify and prioritize the things in their lives that make them content, the things that bring them joy, the things that bring them health. It makes them better in all areas of their lives if they have balance in the things that are most important to them.

Leaders who drift too far away from any part of their lives that give them fulfillment will eventually burn out. If they lose touch with their lives outside of their immediate responsibilities, then they miss what could be making them happy because they spend too much time in the office, attending meetings, squeezing in one more business trip or one more hour answering emails. It's easy to get sucked in to that trap. It takes a certain amount of courage to say, "No, I am going home now," or "I am not going to return that phone call while I'm on vacation with my family. It can wait."

Leadership is a constant balancing act. We balance what needs to be done now, what's urgent, against what's important long-term and what's important in our personal lives. These days, achieving that tenuous balance is harder than ever. We have smart phones that enable us to access information instantly from anywhere in the world. We can receive emails from anywhere in the world, text messages from anywhere in the world, twenty-four hours a day, seven days a week. I see so many people now getting lost in the world of their smart devices.

How many times have you been out to dinner and seen a family sitting together, and every single person at the table is looking at a smart phone? How many times have you seen a couple out for dinner, and before the meal is even served, they're both on their smart phones? One person is texting, one person is checking sports scores. I've even received emails from people saying, "I'm sitting in bed and I just want to get this email back to you quickly."

Whatever your personal priorities, you really need to spend time identifying what those aspects of your life are that make you whole. Then, figure out how you are going to fit that into your life.

It's getting extremely difficult to set boundaries, to prioritize, and so for me, it has become more important than ever to find balance in my life as a leader and to set priorities that allow for a healthy and full personal life.

I recommend that you carve out some time when you can concentrate and give this some serious consideration. Write down the most important aspects of your life. Obviously, you've got to be successful at work. Most people would consider family a top priority. I most certainly do. I personally take my health very seriously. I decided a long time ago that if you work for thirty or forty years, and then you have health issues that keep you from enjoying your retirement because you neglected your health, maybe focusing that much on your career for all those years wasn't the best idea.

I prioritize my health at the top of my daily to-do list because I believe that if you're not healthy, none of the rest of your priorities are going to matter. Six days a week, I spend an hour or more, minimum, exercising. I don't want to spend all these years striving for professional success and then find out I can't spend time with my family in my retirement because I've neglected my health for too long.

Many people prioritize their spiritual lives, their hobbies, or nonprofit organizations. Whatever your personal priorities, you really need to spend time identifying what those aspects of your life are that make you whole. Then, figure out how you are going to fit that into your life. Once a week, I look at my calendar to make sure I'm spending time doing those things that make me happy and whole. Aside from daily exercise, it usually involves finding time to spend with my family. I have children in Australia, and I try to have a video conference with them as often as I can. I send them text messages every day. I send them emails. We schedule family time together with our big extended family once a month or so. You've got to prioritize the things that make you happy, that make you feel fulfilled, and in my experience, unless you intentionally schedule time for those things, they simply won't happen.

I've heard so many leaders say, "If I just get through this year, then next year I'm going to start exercising," or "I want to spend more time with my family, but in these next ninety days I really need to focus on this project." We've all done it—we put off until next month or next year some big goal or dream or desire, but when that time comes, we put it off again. The time to start doing what makes you happy is now because next year is always next year. It rarely becomes this year.

We also need to have the courage to set boundaries when we *are* spending time with friends and family, especially since we have to work so hard to find that time. I'm not perfect at this. I certainly break the rules now and then, but we do our best in our home to have boundaries. When we sit down to a meal, we don't allow cell phones. I don't want someone checking emails or texting friends or checking the sports scores. In all honesty, I'm probably the one who breaks the rules the most, especially when someone calls about an urgent work issue.

We're conditioned to answer the phone when we hear it ring. It has become an automatic response, but the people sitting there in the room with you have made a commitment to be there and spend time with you. Answering the phone is almost insulting. They're talking to you face-to-face and suddenly, you don't want to talk to them because your phone has made a noise. You're acting as if you'd rather talk to the person who's calling you. That's just rude, but we're so conditioned to it. At a minimum, we check to see who is calling to make sure it isn't someone important enough for us to want to ignore the people who are in the room with us.

We do the same with texts. How often do we glance at our phone the second we hear that text come in? Every moment we look down at our phones, we're ignoring the people right there in front of us and sending a powerful message that we care more about who's on the phone than who's beside us. We need to set boundaries with our personal time just like we do with our personal space.

I suggest setting a time when you shut your phone down for the night. In my family, we try to shut them down around eight o'clock. My wife, as the owner of her own consulting firm, always has clients wanting information from her. People she works with constantly want answers from her. The question, "If I answer this, will it get someone else's work going faster?" never ends. There's always another email.

There's always another text message. There's always information out there you'd like to have, but you've got to set boundaries or your personal life will suffer, and you won't be as happy and fulfilled day-to-day. We know this is true for us, so after eight o'clock, we shut things down and spend time doing things that are important to us, even if it's just watching a favorite TV show together or chatting about life, having a glass of wine, and catching up on the day. We know, at that point in the day, every day, we have each other's undivided attention.

We both travel for work, so we're not always there at eight o'clock at night. Our rule is that when you're on the road, knock yourself out. You can work day and night, you can email or text all night long, but when you're with your friends and family, treat them like they're important to you. Let them know just how important they are by not doing any work. Focus on just them. They will feel as valued as they truly are to you, and you will find it easier to maintain those all-important personal relationships in your life. Don't let your career come between you and the people you care about most.

Also, as a leader, you should schedule time to unplug as completely as you can. My wife and I try to find time at least once a quarter—a long weekend, a vacation—for just the two of us, completely away from all work and technology. We get away from the text messages and the cell phone calls and the emails and the social media pages, and we spend time together. We talk about the things we're doing and about what we might want to do differently. We talk about what we might want to do in the future. We kind of level-set. We ask ourselves, "Are we living the lives we want to live or should we be doing something differently?"

When we take the time to ask these questions, we always discover that we need to make some modifications. Typically, we discover that we've over-committed ourselves to other people or projects. We continue to squeeze too many obligations into our lives and we don't have enough time to unwind, unplug, decompress, and take the breath we need to keep our mental health in order. I'm currently very interested in the data coming out about the connection between mental health and rest, making sure your brain is getting all the stimulus it needs and then the rest it needs to keep functioning properly. I'm certainly no expert in this area, but it's becoming more and more important to me to give my body and mind time to unwind, recover, and heal. I won't be surprised if the scientific findings one day show that the top priority people should have to maintain their health is to get more rest.

A few years ago, when I first took on the assignment leading Hallmark's Walmart business, I was so busy putting together a new team, getting new people on board, and learning how to get into a rhythm with this big customer, I don't think we had a weekend or a vacation that wasn't interrupted by a business crisis of some kind. It was very common in the middle of a week's vacation, to be summoned to northwest Arkansas to deal with an issue.

Leaders should not have to be called upon to do that, and those sorts of interruptions will become the rare exception if you've got a great team in place and a great process laid out, but that can be difficult to achieve. You need to come as close to this ideal as you can. Back then, when I was often called away from vacations, my wife figured out a solution to prevent this. She started planning for our vacations to take place out of the country, typically on a cruise ship. When I get on a cruise ship, I'm not going to be looking at many text messages or making many phone calls. I might have to read a few emails, but she allows me to read emails every other day for fifteen minutes during a cruise. The best part is that I'm certainly not going to be able to fly off to Arkansas—or anywhere else for that matter—from the middle of the ocean. In her brilliance, she made me entirely unreachable. We even traveled to Europe once during a very tough time in our business. She could tell I needed a break, so she reminded me, "You're not going to be any good if you don't get away."

Her wisdom helped me navigate through those tough times, and today, my team rarely has those kinds of issues because we've gotten our process in place to deal with problems as they arise. In fact, I can't remember the last time I had to rush to northwest Arkansas to deal with a crisis. Most of those issues are taken care of as we work, before they reach crisis level.

Another helpful practice I've adopted that you might find beneficial is a quick technique for staying in contact with my kids. The company I work for makes, among other things, greeting cards. When my oldest daughter started college at eighteen, I decided to send her a greeting card every Monday. Every week, occasion or not, I sent her a card. Sometimes I would write a little note or sometimes I would include a small gift card. A couple of years later when my son went off to college, I started doing the same for him. Three years later, my younger daughter left for college, and I began the same ritual for her.

My oldest is now thirty-four, my son is thirty-two, and my younger daughter is twenty-nine, and I still send them each a card every week, so my oldest daughter has received at least fifty-two cards a year from me for the last sixteen years. I just say, "Hey, it's Dad, I hope things are going well," or I write something silly. It's just my way of saying that even though I have a busy life and there's a lot going on and my mind's in all sorts of places, I'm always here for you. I send cards to my grandchildren, too, and while we still have a sixteen old at home, I don't send her cards yet, but believe me, when she leaves for college in a couple of years, the ritual will continue.

More recently, I also started sending my children a text message every day. This is one way that technology has enhanced my personal life rather than intruded upon it. Every morning, they each get a little text, including my sons-in-law and my daughter-in-law. I add some little emojis, something specific to each of them. It's just my way of saying, "Dad's here. I'm just a text away." Even my son and daughter-in-law who are in Australia still get a text every day. All of them usually respond, too (mostly every day). It's those little things that keep us connected and keep the bond going even across time and miles, and I know they especially appreciate my efforts when they're dealing with tough times.

Most of this chapter has been about how to achieve and maintain personal balance, but as a business leader, it's important to establish balance in the workplace, too. I see leaders get so immersed in their own categories, their own businesses, their own processes, that they don't spend nearly enough time asking what else is going on in the marketplace.

Years ago, I was vice president of category management. It was common to take market tours for two or three days, so as I was putting a team together and teaching my new people about our responsibilities, we would often tour the marketplace. I gave each person on the team a different shopping assignment as we went into a store. I might say to someone on my team, "In this store, you're a Hispanic woman who is looking for a specific health care item." I might say to someone else, "You are a twenty-five-year-old African American female and you're looking for a specific skin care product."

I assigned everyone the roles of different shopper demographics and directed them to look for specific products in the store and buy them. The retail experience is not complete until the shopper purchases the product. Some new people were amazed at what they discovered in terms of how highly effective some brands were at communicating their product identity with packaging and merchandizing and then what the price for the product was when they checked out. Other products were incredibly hard to find. If you were a Hispanic female who did not speak English as your primary language, it might be nearly impossible to find the right health care product for your child because it wasn't labeled or signed clearly enough for you to find it. My team learned a great deal about what was happening in the marketplace by looking at it through the eyes of a shopper different than they.

I'm in the consumer products business and we spend our time with retailers, but I believe this concept applies to other businesses as well. You need to go and see what other people in your industry are doing. You need to walk the store. Not only your department, but walk the whole store. Walk up and down the aisles. Look at end caps, look at feature displays, go to the grocery aisle, go to electronics -- because everyone has the same challenge. You've got to communicate your product's features and benefits at the right price to a shopper as effectively as you can. As a leader, you need to get outside of your own mind, your own comfort zone, and look at the world through another lens.

I see leaders get so immersed in their own categories, their own businesses, their own processes, that they don't spend nearly enough time asking what else is going on in the marketplace.

Several years ago, I worked for an incredibly strong leader. She left the company to join the academic world, and about three months after she left, we had lunch. During the conversation, I asked her what life was like outside the corporate world. I remember her reply, "Did you know you can pay at the pump? You can actually buy gas, and pay for it at the pump, without having to go inside the gas station to the register."

I wasn't sure if she was serious, "Yes," I stammered, "I've been doing that forever." This technology had been around for many years by then, but she and her husband were high level executives who drove company cars that got cleaned and gassed up for them during the work day, so she truly had no idea. She continued, "I went to a movie the other day, and did you know they have these great big reclining seats that you can lounge in?"

As a leader, you need to get outside of your own mind, your own comfort zone, and look at the world through another lens.

She continued to talk about all these common things that were happening in the world that regular people knew about and used every day. She didn't know because for many years she had been so hyper-focused on her specific assignment that she was missing how everyone else was living their lives. She was so intent on what she was doing that she didn't open her eyes up to the rest of the world. My world *is* consumer goods. If I don't have time to be a consumer of goods, then I'm losing touch. I must keep my finger on the pulse of how people engage with the world.

To be a great leader, you must have balance. You need to identify those aspects of your life that are important to you, that make you whole. You must prioritize them and spend time on them regularly so that your career doesn't overtake your life and cause you to burn out.

As a business leader, you must balance your own professional perspective by looking at the marketplace through the eyes of someone who is different than you—a different shopper, a different category, a different ethnicity, a different retailer. Learn what other people are doing, learn what you need to be doing. This wider point of view will make you better able to make good decisions quickly and confidently. Make maintaining this balance a regular part of your job.

For Reflection

What is most important in your life? What makes it difficult for you to maintain balance in your personal life? What boundaries do you already have in place to help achieve that balance? What additional boundaries do you need to put in place? What is something you've always wanted to do but put off because you felt like you did not have the time? Professionally, what do you do to get out of your own little bubble and see the bigger picture? What more could you do?

Clarity

Leadership requires clarity. This does not always come naturally to people, and although it is closely tied to one's communication skills, it is more than that. Clarity involves our thought processes, our self-perception, and our ability to manage and motivate others. It has much to do with how we see things—the world, our business, and our role in each. Some leaders prefer vagueness. In my experience, the more vague you are, the more friction you create. Choose to think, work, act, and communicate clearly, and everyone wins.

Chapter 15

Build Your Brand

Your personal "brand" is *the* thing these days. It won't take you long if you search through business journals or websites to find people asking, "What's your brand?" The use of the word "brand" to describe a person's professional reputation wasn't used when I was a young businessperson. We called it "character," so I look at a person's individual brand as his or her character. It is the cornerstone of a leader's credibility, and it is demonstrated by the series of choices he or she makes daily.

One steamy, summer Friday evening several years ago, I was getting ready to leave the office around six-thirty. Most people had already headed home, so the parking garage was relatively empty. As I approached my car, I saw that I had a flat tire. "Oh man!" I thought to myself. I was driving a big Suburban that I'd only had a few months, and I had no idea how to change the tire. Reluctantly, I pulled the manual from the glove box and started trying to figure it out.

After only a few minutes, Dave Hall, the head of HR at the time, drove up. "What's goin' on?" he asked casually. As he got out of his car in his suit and tie and white shirt, I explained my problem, and in the blazing heat of the parking garage, he helped me put on the spare tire. It took almost forty-five minutes, and by the end, we were both drenched in sweat and filthy from our endeavors. The whole time, I kept asking myself, "Who would do this?" Dave Hall is the grandson of the company's founder. He didn't have to stop that evening, much less, take the time to roll up his sleeves and help me out. The fact that he *did* speaks volumes about his brand.

Again, several years after that incident, I was shocked to see him standing in the hospital waiting room after my daughter was hit by a car. He offered me a key to his house, which was just minutes from the hospital, and asked, "What can I do to make all of this easier for you?" He continued, "Anything you need from me, just ask."

Our character is evident from the moment we walk in the door. It shows in the way we treat others, the way we handle pressure, the way we make decisions.

I know who Dave Hall is as a person—I know his "brand"—not because he told me, but because he has demonstrated it over and over. His decisions and choices are congruent with what he says, and although I don't always agree with his decisions and choices, I know where he's coming from, and therefore, I trust his judgment. I believe in him and support him.

It has been my experience that the people who most often show up in your life in times of crisis or crossroads are the people with whom you work alongside day in and day out, the people who see who you really are based on the choices you make every single day. Our character is evident from the moment we walk in the door. It shows in the way we treat others, the way we handle pressure, the way we make decisions. If we, as leaders, display solid character, if we work hard every day to do the right thing, we will amass much more than success and have way more than mere colleagues—we will have friends who are there for us and support us, especially in times of need.

Character is developed over time and is the sum of countless decisions, big and small. It's not like you can drive through the fast food window and shout into the microphone, "I'd like a number four reputation, please, small fries, and a diet soda." It doesn't come that easily. Your brand is the cumulative result of all the choices you made yesterday, the ones you're going to make tomorrow, and the ones you're going to make next week, and so on. H. Jackson Brown, author of *Life's Little Instruction Book*, said it perfectly:

> *Good character is more to be praised than outstanding talent. Most talents are, to some extent, a gift. Good character, by contrast, is not given to us. We have to build it, piece by piece—by thought, choice, courage, and determination.*

The first thing you need to determine regarding your character, or brand, is the character traits that are most important to you. If you go to your search engine of choice and type in "character," you'll find an expansive list of traits and an exhaustive range of definitions. One such search yielded a list of well over one-hundred character traits—traits like *ambitious*, *bright*, *bossy*, *charming*, *cautious*, *cooperative*, and so on. Decide what character traits are valuable to you.

I was very fortunate early in my career, in my late twenties, to have a leader who inspired me and took an interest in me. He took a little extra time to help me shape my leadership skills and encouraged me to start drafting answers to these two questions:

1.) What are the ten things that are most important to me?

2.) What am I going to aspire to?

I wrote down ten things. This list became the start of what I consider my brand. Now, honestly, do I do all those things every day? No. Have I flown out of formation or crossed a boundary a few times? Of course. Lots of times. Hundreds of times, but it's important to clearly define the traits you are striving to model as a guideline to keep you on track, and when necessary, get you back on track. If your brand, the reputation of your character in a professional setting, is built over time, it can withstand a few mistakes. A strong personal brand is durable. It can weather office politics, personnel changes, and company downturns. It is the most important component of any leader's philosophy in my opinion. It's about your behavior at work, your leadership. It's about your accountability, and I believe accountability and character are inseparable in a professional setting.

A strong personal brand is durable. It can weather office politics, personnel changes, and company downturns.

You need to set your personal compass clearly toward those behavior traits that are important to you and that you believe you can deliver against. Think of the kind of businessperson you want your customers, your peers, your leaders to think of when they look at you. You want them to know they can count on you for those behaviors you've come to realize are important to you.

An important element of *my* "brand," for instance, is my belief that a leader must follow through. Follow through on everything you say you're going to do, with excellence. Excellence does not mean perfection. Perfection is too expensive. You don't have time or resources to be perfect. Simply put, do the best you can and move on. I have always thought that accomplishing ten goals at ninety-five percent is better than accomplishing five goals at ninety-eight percent. It's just not worth the extra tiny step toward perfection that would cost you the time it would take to accomplish those additional goals, but one hundred percent of the time, you need to do what you say you're going to do, on time, complete, and exactly how you said you would do it, and if you can, take it just a little bit further.

I draw the line at work here, though. I do not bring people's personal choices into consideration as I look at their professional character. I don't factor in a person's life outside of work, whether it's their religious beliefs, political opinions, how they spend their personal time, or who they spend it with. Whatever it might be, it does not impact how I see that person's character in a business setting, and that can be controversial. Some people consider professional and personal character interwoven. I do not. We live in an exceedingly diverse and ever-changing world. I would never begin to say that I understand why a person makes the choices he or she makes. If people are not breaking laws, then it's not my place to judge whatever it is they do outside of work.

Jeff Bezos, the CEO and founder of Amazon once said, "Your brand is what other people say about you when you're not in the room." Nothing says more about your character in the workplace—what the company means to you, what your team means to you—than whether you hold yourself up to this standard. It is crucial to show your team that you hold yourself up to at least the same standard you hold every member of your team.

For Reflection

What does it mean to you to have character? Who do you consider to be a person of character? What are the ten things that are most important to you? What are you going to aspire to? What do you want your team to say about you when you're not in the room?

CHAPTER 16

BE AWARE OF YOUR OWN OPTICS

PERCEPTION IS EVERYTHING, AND you are responsible for your optics within your organization. This means you must be aware of how people see and perceive you as a member of your team, what people think of you and your work style. We might not want to admit it, but optics matter. Others will perceive you based on how you research problems, how often you attend meetings, how quickly you reply to emails, how you grind it out, and how available you are to people when they need you. These are all personal decisions that you are empowered to make most of the time.

Like I've already stated, we are accountable for everything, and I do mean *everything*. I expect people to own their decisions and behaviors about how they dress, whether they are on time, their decisions to work from home or the office, and what ends up as public information on their social media accounts. As a leader, I am accountable for all those things, so I expect my team to be as well. Having a clear, keen sense of how your decisions and actions are perceived will help you be successful.

Work styles are changing rapidly nowadays. People can work effectively from anywhere in the world. They can work on planes, in hotels, and in coffee shops. I've known people who do their very best work sitting in a Starbuck's or a Panera or on an airplane where no one is there to bother them. I understand that. I do some of my best work when I'm out of the office, but people need to own their optics, to understand and be responsible for how their work style is perceived. When someone asks me, "Can I work from home?" my answer is always the same, "You make the choices you want to make, but pay attention to how the people around you are reacting to those choices."

The same holds true for appropriate dress and appearance. When I first started out, a suit and tie were a given, but obviously times have changed, and the scope of what is considered appropriate for work has widened dramatically. I love to go to work in my jeans as much as the next guy, but again, it is important to have a clear understanding of how what you wear and how you look are perceived.

It's been my observation after all these years that people who fly out of formation and are always doing things differently than everybody else tend to stand out negatively over time.

I believe that people should fly in formation with the rest of their team. If the rest of the team dresses casually, you should dress casually. We've come a long way, but every workplace possesses a certain "culture," and like it or not, you need to try to fit the mold. In some offices, collars and ties are still the norm. In others, tattoos or blue hair rule the roost. You need to have your finger on the pulse of the culture, stick to it, and expect your team to do so as well.

It's been my observation after all these years that people who fly out of formation and are always doing things differently than everybody else tend to stand out negatively over time. You must have this visibility in mind and make your work style choices accordingly. I am not saying there is no room for variance or diversity. I *am* saying that if you're too far off the curve, people will notice, and that might be a positive or it might not. Have a clear sense of what you're putting out there and how others are receiving it.

That being said, we are all far more than what others see on the surface. Misperceptions and false impressions happen, so we must be open. I know that sometimes people look at me and assume I'm just another baby-boomer who didn't have to work for my successes. I am a baby-boomer, but I certainly did not come from money, power, or prestige. Nothing was handed to me, and nothing was easy. Once people get to know me, they are often surprised at my background, so as a leader, I must be accountable for my own optics. If I know that people often misperceive me, I have the responsibility to make sure I clearly convey who I really am. Also, as a leader, I have a responsibility to be aware that *my* perceptions of others may not tell the whole story.

For Reflection

How do you think you are perceived in the workplace? Consider the culture and climate of your organization. How closely do you fly in formation? When do you deviate and why? What deviations in others catch your attention?

Chapter 17

What Gets Measured Gets Done

Your job is to handle the responsibilities you're accountable for and accomplish them to the best of your ability. The surest way to do that is to have the metrics in place that tell you if you're moving in the right direction at the right pace to reach your goals. It could be daily metrics, weekly, monthly, quarterly, yearly, or all the above. Use whatever metrics you need at any given time to see if you are on track to meet the goals for which you are accountable. If you have a clear sense of those metrics, and you hold your team accountable for their individual roles along the way, your chances of being successful increase significantly.

I've worked with some brilliant retailers in my day. The most successful ones measure you as a supplier. Walmart is probably the best at this. They measure everything, and even if you don't think they're doing their math right, or you disagree with the metrics they expect of you, the fact that they're measuring you against a clearly defined goal means you're going to work just a little bit harder to meet that goal. As a leader, you should know that what gets measured gets done. Measure it, and people will do it. Be clear up front

> *Be clear up front about what will be measured and how it will be measured, and people will not only do it, but will most often exceed the metrics every time.*

about what will be measured and how it will be measured, and people will not only do it, but will most often exceed the metrics every time.

It is also extremely important for a leader to keep the team focused on the goals at hand. It's easy to get distracted by new ideas and initiatives, so you, as the leader, must stay on task and steer your team's efforts in the right direction, making sure they align with the defined business goals. It is *those* goals, after all, that you are responsible for meeting.

Sometimes a team member will come to me with an idea. Maybe he or she just attended a seminar or talked to someone respected in another industry. New ideas are great, but I always ask the critical question, "Is this idea on strategy?" If not, then it's not an idea we can afford to spend our time and resources on.

Another issue is when someone comes to me with a problem, and I realize it's an internal problem, something unique to our company or our own corporate culture, that has nothing to do with anything outside the building. Again, I am compelled to ask some critical questions, "Did it come from the marketplace? Does it affect our current direction toward our goals?" If not, then it's just a group of coworkers talking about something going on in the building, and I don't need to hear about it. I want to hear about what's going on in the marketplace. The issues that are relevant and important to the forward progress of our work start in the marketplace, not within the walls of the office.

Sometimes the market can swing or our goals can change, and we must make changes to realign with those new goals. Sometimes those changes can be sudden and drastic, and this can make the team feel uncertain about the work they're doing if they're asked to drastically change how they approach the business. However, if the overall strategy is consistent and predictable, say, we've got to increase our percentage of square footage at Walgreens, knowing what we know today, is this on strategy to meet that goal? Yes? Then, even if it's different from what we were doing yesterday, it's still on strategy, and it will still make sense to the team.

If your leadership style is predictable, and your team feels like they can trust how you will react because you have proven to them over time what you expect from them and what they can expect from you, they will have confidence in you as a leader to guide them forward.

For Reflection

Are you more, or less likely to accomplish something if you know your performance will be measured? What metrics in your industry get measured? Are there things that don't get measured that should? How would you propose measuring them?

CHAPTER 18

STOP THE DRAMA

DRAMA WILL DERAIL A leader. It will derail a team. It will waste resources and potentially cost you your job. You must, as a leader, be aware of negative tension if it builds up on your team and put a stop to it immediately and entirely. I've observed many leaders over time, and I've seen drama derail them. I've worked with many feisty customers, customers who get in your face, and I've seen many salespeople who meet with this sort of customer and get worn down. Maybe they've had a bad sales week or month, or deliveries weren't on time, or any number of mistakes were made, and this sort of bad outcome just eats the salesperson alive.

Some retailers can be confrontational and hard to deal with. When sales leaders get their bell rung by an angry customer, sometimes they might feel like they need to come back to the home office and yell at everybody else. Whoever else they see as accountable, they just beat them down, and soon, no one wants to deal with that leader.

Instead, effective leaders deal with their own frustrations. Do not pass them on. I remember when I hired an incredibly strong leader a few years ago. She had twenty years of experience under her belt and was highly regarded, but she had a reputation for sometimes being too harsh with her team. One day, I had to tell her, "Look, we're going to have times when we fall short and you're going to get frustrated. Your job is *not* to make everybody else feel your pain. Your job is to take it, to understand it, to make sure you know what the issue is. If you need to go home that night and ride your exercise bike, go for a run, watch a movie, drink a glass of wine, then go ahead. Whatever you need to do, do it, but your job is not to derail the rest of the organization by spreading that tension all over the office. Sleep on it. Figure out what we're going to do, call me, and let's talk about what we need to do to move forward."

I can't tell you how many times I've seen leaders pass along the drama. When leaders allow themselves to do this, when they believe their job is to ignore it or even add to it because of their own frustration, or if they don't realize that this is what they're doing, they have failed as leaders.

Empower your team members to work it out themselves and help to facilitate a process of open and direct communication between the people involved.

Too many times, leaders get caught up in the drama between people on their teams. If somebody comes to them with an issue about somebody else, rather than saying, "Go talk to that person," they get involved. They might say, "Let me talk to a few more people and see what sort of solution I can come up with." What they're doing is adding to the drama. You just need to stop it as soon as it presents itself to you. Empower your team members to work it out themselves and help to facilitate a process of open and direct communication between the people involved. This aligns with my work style I mentioned in an earlier chapter. When leaders involve themselves in the drama, they make it bigger and prolong it. They allow their team to get distracted, waste time, and the business suffers. Ultimately, the leader is the one responsible for allowing this to happen.

I guarantee you that if a leader asks a team member, "Have you ever had an issue with this other person?" most people are going to answer affirmatively because of something that happened at some point in the past, and all this is going to do is stir up more drama. When leaders play into the drama, what they are really demonstrating is that they've lost skills and they've lost focus.

I had the opportunity to work for one individual several times in my career. Initially, I worked for him early in my career, and we had a great relationship. He hired me onto a couple of his other teams along the way, and he was an outstanding manager early in his career and became a strong leader, a very respected, credible leader. In his last five years or so, however, he fell into the trap of promoting drama. For whatever reason, he changed. He lost his focus. He became jaded. He turned into someone who spent his time talking about what was wrong with the business and about things we could not change.

All we can do is work on the assignments we are responsible for and be accountable for the results of our work. We each need to do the best we can every day and follow through with excellence, but this individual lost his ability to do that. Eventually, he turned into the person who was creating drama. More and more frequently, he found ways to distract the organization with his complaints and his growing list of what he saw as unfixable problems. This behavior finally led to his departure from the company. I literally watched this man walk out of the building late one night with a cardboard box in his hands, get in his car, and drive away.

This was someone who was highly respected for years and years. I thought that when he left the company, when he retired, we were going to have a banquet for him. We would celebrate him, but none of that happened, and it was solely because he lost his focus on the business and stopped actively maintaining the skills needed to deal with these sorts of issues.

Leaders stop the drama. Your job is to not get involved in it in an effort to help. Your job is not to ignore it because you feel you have more important things to do. Your job is not to pass it along because you're tired of dealing with it. Your job is to stop it.

For Reflection

Drama happens. Think about an instance of workplace drama that was handled expediently. How was it handled? Think of an instance where it was allowed to fester. What were the results? How do you see yourself, as a leader, putting a stop to drama?

Conviction

Leadership requires conviction. You must be certain of at least SOME things, convinced of their validity or truth, and then willing to go all in for those things. For me, I believe that the marketplace tells all—you must understand it to be successful. I believe that the best team always wins. I believe that leadership happens top to bottom, and I believe that you must have passion for the future. These are the things about which I am certain in business, the things I am convinced are true. Find what those things are for you and stick to your guns. Others may not always agree with your convictions, but a person of conviction always garners great respect.

Chapter 19

Understand the Marketplace

Many leaders I've observed and worked with are too intensely focused on how their own company works—their operations, their internal politics, the processes they use to move the business forward—that they lose sight of the most important aspect of any business: the marketplace. Understanding the marketplace is crucial to a leader's day-to-day responsibilities because this knowledge is the ultimate filter for decision-making.

The marketplace is the vast and ever-changing world your company needs to exist and thrive. It is the source of any and all income your company and its people will earn, and it is, therefore, the ultimate measure of your company's success. To understand the marketplace, you must understand, with as much depth as possible, what *your* market is, how it is defined, and the dynamics that make up the marketplace in your industry.

When I consider the dynamics of my marketplace, I separate those dynamics into four categories: shoppers, consumers, competitors, and customers. Shoppers are the people who are in the stores looking to buy goods. When considering shoppers, you must become familiar with how they behave in the various retail environments that exist today.

For example, in my industry, I examine how shoppers buy our goods in a drug store, in a convenience channel, in a big box retailer, and online. Trust me, those are very different marketplaces, and shoppers behave differently in them.

Consumers are the people who could benefit by the purchase of your product or service, but are not yet in the retail environment shopping for it. When considering your consumers, you must identify consumer trends and familiarize yourself with current consumer insights—how do consumers want to buy your goods and services differently than they used to and what's driving them to think this way?

The next dynamic to consider in the marketplace is your competitors. I've never been an advocate for copying a competitor. I think that's a ridiculous business plan. It doesn't take much horsepower or talent to see what a competitor is doing and then try to do that, too. Although it appears that some companies do just that, all it guarantees is that you will remain behind your competition in meeting any new trend the marketplace reveals that could be capitalized on.

I *do* believe you need to intentionally keep your finger on the pulse of your competition and know what they're doing. When considering your competition, find out what their new products are and what their current pricing is. What does their distribution look like? What customers are they targeting? This knowledge is power. It equips you to make smarter decisions and hopefully come out on top of your competition.

The most important dynamic of the marketplace to consider is your individual customers—in our case they are the retailers we sell our products to. You must understand what's going on with your customers from the executive level all the way down to the buying level. Many people believe that if you have strong executive relationships, CEO to

CEO, president to president, senior VP to senior VP, all will be great with the relationship between those two companies. It has been my experience that those relationships are important in that they allow you to have the critical conversations at the critical times, but you have to make sure you're providing what the purchasing group wants you to provide. A buyer, somebody above a buyer, an individual merchandise leader—those people are important to serve properly, because those people have metrics, specific financial goals they are required to meet. It is your job to provide relevant products or services that will allow them to meet their goals.

Understanding the marketplace is something I stress to my teams constantly. I want everyone to possess knowledge deep and wide about the inner workings of the market.

If you're helping those people at the buyer level make their numbers, if you're making them happy, and if you have the relationships at the top level, then you've found the sweet spot in your relationship with that customer. You must develop and maintain all those relationships. You can't have one but not the other. If you only have relationships at the buying level, you're never going to break through with the bigger ideas and create the kind of change that leads to real growth. On the other hand, if you only have relationships at the executive level, and you're not making the buying group happy, then you're going to have day-to-day problems that keep you from achieving your more immediate goals. Both relationships are critical.

Understanding the marketplace is something I stress to my teams constantly. I want everyone to possess knowledge deep and wide about the inner workings of the market. It's the lifeblood of our business. I've even discovered that using the marketplace in the interview process can be an invaluable tool to gauge prospective team members. Once, when

I was hiring category managers, which at the time was a relatively new role, I interviewed a gentleman who told me he had re-invented the entire Campbell's Soup merchandising plan. I asked him to meet me in the pet food aisle of the nearest Wal-Mart. I said, "Tell me what you see," and much to my surprise, he could not say much of anything. For someone who supposedly re-invented the way a huge brand is merchandized on the grocery store shelves, he demonstrated little insight into merchandizing concepts. He clearly did not understand the marketplace.

I invited another prospect for the same job to go through the same exercise, and immediately, he began to articulate the reasons behind the placement of various products at various levels—higher profit margin items in front and at eye level, heavier bags of pet food on the lower shelves to make it easier for shoppers to lift, etc. He literally took the aisle apart piece by piece. I then took him to the snack aisle, where he proceeded to do the same thing, noting how it was arranged function vs. brand and how the dips were placed adjacent to the chips they were meant to be used with. Clearly, *he* understood the marketplace, and he got the job.

My belief in the primacy of understanding the market is firmly rooted in years of experience. I am convinced that this deserves much of my time and attention and that it is worth my team's time and attention as well. This conviction drives a great deal of my thought-processes daily, and I would venture a guess that it does so for most successful leaders, no matter the industry. Invest in understanding *your* marketplace, and many problems will be solved.

For Reflection

How do you define your industry's marketplace? Who are your shoppers and how do they behave? Who are your consumers? What are the consumer trends you're paying attention to? Who is your competition? Do you know what they've been up to lately? If not, how can you find out? Who are your customers? How would you describe the relationships with your customers? Are there areas that need improvement?

Chapter 20

The Best Team Wins

If you have a clear leadership philosophy and you know how to leverage that philosophy to create a winning culture, the next step is to build the best team.

Every leader must grow accustomed to and comfortable with the one constant in business—change. You're given new assignments, you work in an ever-changing marketplace, and you will be called upon to build a new team many times throughout your career. Building a solid team is the starting point for any leader.

You must know the range of skills you require to meet your goals, and you must have the relationships in your organization that allow you to find and hire the best people you can. Experienced leaders know that their reputations precede them, and so if you want to attract the best people to your organization, you must have an established reputation as a strong and reliable leader. If you focus every day on consistently following a set of principles, and those principles align with your company's goals and your personal beliefs, then over time, you will build

> *The best leaders spend a significant amount of their time making sure they have the best team in place to meet their goals at that time. The best leaders have a passion for coaching.*

a reputation as a strong leader, and you will attract the right people to work for you.

A diverse, engaged, and skilled team will consistently win, meaning you will meet your objectives and foster the best relationships with your customers over a long period of time. Corporate strategies and corporate leaders will come and go. There will be years when you have great products, stellar marketing programs, a smooth and efficient supply chain, and then inevitably, there will be years when those things do not happen. The product will not sell as well as you hoped it would, the marketing programs will fall flat, the supply chain will break down, the economy will slow, and retailers will have their own problems that result in negative effects on your business. There will be tough years, but if you have the best team, you will win consistently over time.

Many leaders do not spend enough time developing their teams. Instead, they spend too much time managing up, making sure the people above them know all the things they are doing. The best leaders spend a significant amount of their time making sure they have the best team in place to meet their goals at that time. The best leaders have a passion for coaching.

As a leader, you have depths of experience and skills upon which you can draw to help your team. When team members have one-on-one time with you, encourage them to bring a list of the choices they are facing. They don't need to spend time sharing with you how they came to their choices, but if they're looking at a fork in the road, they should be able to list what the plusses and minuses are, the pros and cons of those options, and based on your experience as a leader, you should be able to guide them toward which option might have the most risk and which one might have the most reward.

As you develop your team, help your people leverage their strengths. Seventy percent of their time should be spent working in areas where they are strongest and working on improving upon those strengths. Another twenty percent of their time should be spent trying to improve upon the skill sets they should have, but need to further develop. They may need growth in communication skills or technical skills or whatever the case may be. The remaining ten percent of their time will likely be spent performing tasks that involve skills they're never going to master.

If a team member is not skilled at ten percent of their job, I do not think a leader should try to force improvement in those areas. The ten percent of skills a person is not proficient in will likely stay at ten percent. As a leader, when you're trying to build your best team, you take the strengths of your people and magnify them, you add some new skills, and you minimize their flat spots. Everybody is going to have flat spots. Don't spend an inordinate amount of time trying to help everybody excel at everything.

I learned this lesson early in my career when I'd been with the company seven or eight years and was working for one of the smartest people I'd ever met. During my year-end review, we eventually started talking about areas of improvement. I had written a long list of skills I wanted help developing over time, some financial skills, knowledge about the supply chain, and other areas of the business with which I was not yet very familiar. His response surprised me. Essentially, he said, "You're never going to be good at that. You're trying to understand areas that are outside your skill set. I don't want you spending your time trying to become average at understanding the supply chain when you could be spending that time becoming even better at the areas in which you already excel. I want you to know who to go to for those sorts of

As you're developing your people, help them to become better at those skills they're already good at and help them manage their flat spots by showing them how to find out where to go to get help in those areas when they need it.

answers when you need them. You just need to know who to ask when a question in that area arises. You're not going to need to know everything. Just know who *does* know it. Here are the things you're good at. Let's leverage those to their maximum, and let's find a way to cover your flat spots."

That was an enlightening conversation for me to have as a relatively young manager because other leaders I had worked for expected me to know the answer to every single question. It was almost like a challenge or a game to them. I remember when I was a very young individual contributor, I had a boss who would come by my office and ask about reports that he felt like I should know. When I asked other people what that report was, it turned out to be some miniscule, obscure summary of a product that had been out of production for years. It was clearly something I did not need to know. As a young individual contributor, I spent far too much time trying to know everything instead of focusing on the things that were going to make me better, make me different, and make me a leader. The thought of spending time improving in the areas in which I excelled, rather than working tirelessly to become average at everything, was inspiring to me. As you're developing your people, help them to become better at those skills they're already good at and help them manage their flat spots by showing them how to find out where to go to get help in those areas when they need it.

Don't be a leader who just TAKES from your team. It happens, and it's disappointing to watch. I've seen it far too many times—leaders who just take the perks and expect their teams to work ridiculous hours and perform crazy tasks, leaders who feel entitled but are unwilling to give anything back to their teams. In the military, there's a saying, "Soldiers eat first." I love that! If you're a leader who is looking out for your team and who truly wants your team to be successful, let them eat first, so to speak. I believe that you should learn something from every boss you work under. You should leave every assignment with a few more arrows in your quiver. As leaders, it is our responsibility to make sure we coach and teach our teams so that they go on to future assignments better for having worked for us.

To create a winning culture on your team, it is important to foster a culture of approval, rather than a culture of criticism.

As you lead your team and develop your people, collect a breadth of experiences and bring together a group of people who are going to challenge you and each other. I want a team that looks differently and thinks differently than me. I want diversity—diversity of thought, diversity of experiences, diversity of skill sets. I want a team that is willing to debate, so I empower them to do so. As a leader, I know that at some point I have to stop the debate and make a decision, but I give my team the latitude to disagree. This helps everyone to grow.

To create a winning culture on your team, it is important to foster a culture of approval, rather than a culture of criticism. What I mean by "a culture of approval" is that I expect my team to make mistakes. If you are not making mistakes, you are not pushing hard enough. I'm not talking about the mistakes that are made when something is being ignored or someone isn't paying attention. Acceptable mistakes are mistakes of aggression. I want my team members to push hard, I want them to make a mistake, and if they learn from it, then that's okay. If they keep making the same mistake, that's different, but I would rather have a team I can coach on how to make fewer mistakes while being aggressive than a team I need to coach on how to be aggressive in the first place.

Leaders should be strict with strategy, but sensitive with people. As a leader, it is your job to set the strategy and then provide your people with the necessary tools to accomplish the goals set for them. Of course, they're going to make mistakes, but most people can learn and are extremely coachable, if given a chance.

I expect excellence from my team, but not perfection. I've never understood leaders who say things like, "We are going to execute our plan perfectly this quarter," or "We are going to launch this new program flawlessly." There is no such thing as *perfect* or *flawless* in my opinion. If a team ends up executing a program perfectly, then chances are they spent too much time on it. If you spent too much time in development, then you didn't get it to market fast enough.

Of course, there are numerous examples where perfection (or near perfection) *is* critical. I'm not referring to those instances. I'm not referring to the professionals who are making blood pressure medicines or launching satellites into orbit. Those people probably need to be close to perfect most of the time. I'm referring to the programs that are planned and executed by consumer product and service companies, and in those cases, ninety percent is good enough.

I strongly believe that leaders should reward their people for positive results. Be careful, however, not to reward "busyness," which often masks itself as productivity but is not the same thing. Reward your people when the job gets done and you've made your numbers, but also be careful not to reward too early. I've seen leaders make the mistake of rewarding progress. This kills a team's momentum over time and can result in the adverse effect of damaging morale. You can't reward people for progress. You have to reward them for results, and if you're not having enough celebrations for all the results you're achieving, it may be time to look in the mirror. If your team isn't winning, take a good hard look at yourself before placing blame on everyone else.

The best leaders are always reinventing their teams and recruiting the next people to join their team. The key members of my team usually have a three to four- year window where they do their very best work. After that point, it's my job, as their leader, to make sure they move on to a new assignment or leadership position that is best for them.

Sometimes, people just flatten out after three or four years, but they're doing great work and can continue to do that work on another team. There are also the people who fall short, and it is the leader's role to help them go do something else.

Even with the people who do solid work on your team, there comes a time when you need some fresh thinking. You need a new person with a new perspective. It's your job to make sure that any person you move off your team lands in a positive position on another team. It's likely that another team needs support in that person's area of expertise and he or she could make a positive difference there, could really shine. Your job as a leader is to always put the best team in place and evolve the team over time. This must include helping individuals when it's time for them to move on. This might be your single biggest responsibility to your team members.

<u>For Reflection</u>

What are your strongest skill sets? Where are your flat spots? What does a "winning culture" look like? Think about all the bosses you've worked for—who stands out in your memory as being a particularly good "coach?" What did he/she do to coach you? As a coach yourself, what do you hope to teach your team? Do you see it as your responsibility to help your team move on, when it's time, to bigger and better assignments? Why or why not?

Chapter 21

Lead from Top to Bottom

At least twice a year, a leader should take the time to go top to bottom with each of his or her direct reports. Have them take you through every step of one or two of their biggest projects, or if you have an organization that involves manufacturing and distribution plants, make sure you walk the floor. If you lead a large geographical area, when you're in the marketplace with the sales manager, take a deep dive into their business. Visit accounts. Talk to retailers. Walk every aisle of every department. I try to do this about once a quarter, but at the very least, twice a year. Start at the top—their strategy, their tactics, their initiatives, their metrics. Go as deep as you can into each of those areas until you think you've asked as many questions as possible.

I used to work for a strong leader who was responsible for quite a bit of our subsidiary businesses. At least twice a year, we would do a subsidiary financial review. After the review, he would go into the office and ask five or six people simple questions like, "What's going on? Can you tell me about the new product lines? Can you tell me how you feel about the new benefits program?" Just ask a question or two and people will give you unpolished feedback. If the feedback

> *It's amazing what you can learn if you just ask a few simple questions.*

you hear is in line with the information you received from the strategy review or the financial review, then everything is great.

Sometimes, however, that feedback will not be congruent, and then you know you have a problem. Once, when I asked a worker on the warehouse floor, “What have you been doing lately?” he replied, “We spent the last week moving all the inventory out before you got here.”

“Excuse me, say that again?”

He told me his boss didn’t want me to see all the inventory that had been stacking up in the warehouse, so they were assigned to move it to another location. It’s amazing what you can learn if you just ask a few simple questions.

In another instance, when I was leading a large team, we were running out of key components to complete the installation of new store shelves and merchandizing. I had gone through what I thought were the correct steps from the beginning of the project to avoid this from happening. Did we provide the right forecast? Did we hit our pre-work dates on time? Everything added up, but there was not enough inventory. This would be a major issue if we weren’t able to install the store fixtures the way we agreed with the customer, so I called the woman who oversaw all the manufacturing plants and said, “We’re not getting inventory. What’s going on?”

“I don’t know,” she replied, “but I’ll find out.”

At about five o’clock the next morning, she texted, “I’m driving to the plant. Something doesn’t feel right.” She didn’t want to wait for a flight, so she drove the five hours to the plant, only to find that when she arrived, most of the leaders were out of the office. Some were out to lunch or playing a round of golf, and the line that produced the fixture components we needed wasn’t even running. While she was there, she got the line running, and it didn't take long before everyone started showing up at the plant that afternoon. Obviously, word had gotten out that she was there. At the end of that day, she was airfreighting fixtures to my stores so we could complete the installations. Her quick response and willingness to dig in to identify the problem were great examples of leadership. I'm not sure what happened to the leaders in the plant, but I'm sure it wasn't a good day for them.

On a different occasion, I flew to Baltimore to spend a couple of days with a regional sales person, driving around visiting accounts. I wanted to see how the new product lines were looking and how the new installations were going up. We visited four stores each day, everything looked great, and I couldn't have been happier about the things I saw and the comments I heard from our retail customers.

About three months later, I was back in the area and decided to spend another day with her. We visited the exact same retail customers. Then, I picked a different one and said, "Let's go see this store."

She quickly replied, "That customer is not in today."

"That's okay," I said, "we'll go anyway. And how about this customer?"

Again, a speedy response, "Well, that's a really long drive and there will be a lot of traffic."

I finally convinced her to take me to one of these stores. As soon as we walked in, they immediately exclaimed, "We haven't seen you in months! We've been trying to get ahold of you." After spending some time there and dealing with that, she assured me that this situation was an exception, so I suggested we visit another store we hadn't yet seen together. Guess what? The same thing happened. I told her to take me to yet another store, and the same thing

> *...as the leader, you need to occasionally take a deep dive with even your best people.*

happened there, too. It turned out there were fifteen or so stores she visited all the time because she liked doing business with them, and she simply avoided the rest of her accounts.

I had a similar situation with a senior sales person in South Florida. We were looking at installation floor plans and product shipment dates. This was after my experience in Baltimore, so I was paying more attention to which customers I visited with my sales people. On my first day in Florida, we visited all the stores he chose. On the second day, I picked a store that was not on his list, and not surprisingly, he said, "That's a long drive and there will be a lot of traffic. It'll take all day."

That sounded oddly familiar, so I assured him, "That's okay, these stores stay open until nine o'clock, and I can work back at my hotel late into the night."

We arrived at the store at about seven-thirty, and the sales rep did not know where our department was. We wandered around aimlessly and finally asked a sales associate who directed us upstairs. It turned out that our department had been relocated upstairs for a year-and-a-half, and this salesperson didn't even know it. He turned beet red with embarrassment.

After that, I said, "We've still got some time. Let's go see this other store." When we arrived, the situation was similar. Over the next thirty days it became clear that he was not working, and he moved on.

The point here is that as the leader, you need to occasionally take a deep dive with even your best people. Most leaders will likely run into less dramatic issues than my examples. You'll more often discover smaller problems that can be fixed. There were many situations when I sat down with people and found they were spending time on unimportant tasks or they were redoing parts of our process that didn't need fixing. Sometimes, they thought I had expected certain things from them that I didn't. With minor adjustments, I could help them become more efficient.

As a leader, you need to focus on the big issues, but at least two, and up to four times a year, take a deep dive from top to bottom with all your people to make sure you understand what they're doing and how they're doing it. It is imperative to see how they're spending their time and to ensure that they're focusing on the right aspects of the business. It is equally important to see how you can help them make improvements based on your broader perspective and experience.

For Reflection

Have you ever had a boss take a deep dive with you in your work? If so, describe that experience and consider any positive or negative outcomes of that experience. If not, were there times when that would've been helpful? Have you ever done this as a manager or leader? What did you uncover? In what areas of your business would such a deep dive be the most helpful or necessary?

Chapter 22

Lead Into the Future

Leaders must lead. It sounds so simple, but it's been my experience that what most leaders actually do is *manage*. They were promoted through the ranks because they were good managers, and over time they've become great managers. They're experts at timelines and budgets and interpersonal conflict. They have mastered the skill of keeping their direct reports moving smoothly through their workday, but leaders should not be spending their time managing assigned tasks. It is the role of leaders to define the future. They must make the case for change, convince people to follow them, and create the path that leads them into these new directions. This may sound simple, but multiple barriers within an organization can make change difficult.

Culture is one of the biggest barriers because it is extremely hard to change in a company, but you can create your own winning culture within your team and possibly even change the broader organization through leading by example. There are other barriers, too, such as skill set gaps, unclear decision-making, business model flaws, conflicting objectives, and many others that get in the way of change. It is the leader's role to show what the future looks like and create the path to get there.

I've identified several steps that helped me become a more forward-looking leader and to create my own vision and culture for my team. Obviously, some of these steps will be different for people working within different corporate cultures, but if you embark on this path, I think you will find yourself better equipped to look to the future and lead a team with a winning culture.

If you are in a leadership position, you've earned it. Trust that.

Step 1: Spend time with other leaders who have a vision. This includes people in your company, but also leaders *outside* your company, and I would emphasize outside your company. Find those companies and the leaders within those companies that have a vision and a winning culture and spend time with them. There are many opportunities to do this, attending seminars or joining share groups. Seek out opportunities to spend time with other leaders. Ask them questions, learn from them, and spend time in the marketplace with them. Immerse yourself in their culture. See the world through their eyes.

Step 2: Avoid and eliminate people who hold you back. Avoid spending time with people who keep you from developing a winning culture, who do not share your vision for the future and can't get on board. That does not include people who are trying to help you avoid mistakes or point out issues along the way. That is very different. Those people are trying to support you, but you know there are people not on the same page as you and who are going to hold you back and keep you from creating the culture and vision that you want to achieve. Get them off your team. Take them off your calendar.

Step 3: Surround yourself with people who genuinely want to share your vision. This is the logical next step. Make sure these people have the skills and the desire to help you get there.

Step 4: Focus on the big issues that really matter. Ask everyone on your management team to make a list of all the projects they're working on, and then put them into three columns. The first column is for the big projects that will really move your organization forward if they're executed well and align with your vision. The second column is for the projects that need to get done to run the business, not the big, overarching projects, but the day-to-day tasks that need completing to move the business forward. The third column is for everything else.

Once you've created your columns, stop doing everything listed in the third column. You'll be amazed at how many people spend time on their own pet projects that no one's going to care about and are not going to matter, even if they're done a hundred percent perfectly. Stop that work. It's a waste of time.

Look at the first column, and pick the top three to five items on that list. Invest your time in those projects and push them forward to the very end. Those are the projects that matter, and positive results there are what will make the biggest difference for your team and for your business. I've done this numerous times in my organizations and it's highly effective.

Step 5: Be a fearless leader. If you are in a leadership position, you've earned it. Trust that. Trust your own talent, follow your passion, and silence the fear inside of you. I've seen many leaders who had the skills and passion but were afraid of failure, of not being successful and not making the money they were being called upon to make for their company. Silence those fears. Some person or some organization has put you in a leadership position because you have demonstrated that you have the skills and the drive to do the job. Someone at a high level trusts you, so trust yourself, move forward with confidence, and don't let fear hold you back.

If you *are* fearful, it's important to identify exactly what you are afraid of. Ask yourself that question and make a list of the things you fear in your leadership role. My guess is that the list essentially boils down to failure to make your numbers, but the truth is that if you don't lead, if you don't trust yourself, you're probably not going to be successful in this role anyway, and you should move on to a new assignment. Plan confidently and trust your talent. Make decisions and move forward by acting on them. Fear cripples decision-making and renders us hostages to our own insecurities. We worry far too much about being "wrong" or being fired. All leaders can benefit from freeing themselves from fear.

Step 6: Manage and track how you spend your time. I've seen great leaders do this and even those who ask their administrative assistants to help them with this. They accurately track how much time they spend leading vs. managing vs. administrating. If you're not spending fifty percent of your time leading, then you've got a problem. Leading can be spending time with other leaders, spending time with other organizations, or sharing your vision with your own organization. If you spend half of your time leading your organization, people will follow you. If you find yourself spending more than half your time managing and administrating, then you need to make the proper adjustments to your priorities to make sure you're spending enough of your time leading.

You must be able to think of leadership as a chess match rather than a game of checkers.

Every Sunday, I sit down with a cup of coffee and look at my schedule for the week. I assess what I need to do versus what I want to do, and then I look at how much time I am devoting to those various things. I am intentional about making time for the things that are important to me. If it is a priority, then plan for it. Make time for it. This includes personal things like making time to exercise as well as making time to really *lead* your team.

Step 7: Look around the corners. I've always loved this phrase. It means to understand what the next four or five steps are going to look like once you've made your decision. You must be able to think of leadership as a chess match rather than a game of checkers. You must have an opinion based on your experience and knowledge about what's going to happen. Once you make a decision and implement your plan in the marketplace, you must be prepared to act accordingly. Sometimes you need to act quickly. Sometimes you need to let a situation ride itself out. Sometimes you need to make multiple choices at once, but you must look around the corners and think critically about what likely lies ahead for your business. It means being proactive, rather than reactive, and the ability to do this well comes with experience. After some trial and error, you will have the confidence to know that if I do *this*, then *that* is going to happen.

Step 8: Make the news, don't report it. A senior vice president at Kmart once told me this, and I have come to appreciate his wisdom. Leaders must make things happen and inspire the organization to follow. They must *make* the news. They must be so busy doing what they need to do that being the first to report it has no value. A warning sign of a poor leader is one who is always reporting the news, always looking in the rear-view mirror and telling everyone around them what has already happened. You don't need a leader who reports what happened already. Leaders define future outcomes, they share the steps they've mapped out that they want their team to take. They're making decisions and communicating those decisions, and they're moving forward. Look to the future and create your own headlines.

Step 9: Find the friction. When I gather my team, I ask, "Where's the friction?" and "How do you deal with it?" For each project they're working on, I want to know what's holding them back and what's going on that might keep them from moving forward

It might be a support organization that's not moving as quickly as we thought it would. It might be they don't have the budget they need to continue making progress. It might be a supply chain issue. It might be unclear who is making the decisions. As a leader, you must find the friction and you must make it go away so your team can move forward.

Step 10: Ask yourself, "When did I have the most passion in my career?" When you were coming up the ladder and you had multiple assignments, either with the company you're with today or with a previous company, when did you have the most passion? Do you remember what it felt like? Did you work for someone who inspired you? Did you have a great team around you that motivated you? Did you work in an environment with a great culture that made you want to win every day? Answer those questions. I find it helpful to write them down, and then, recreate that experience for your team. Visualize everyone on your team having the same passion you had when you were coming up the ladder and you were inspired. If you can recreate that, great things can happen on your team.

One of the responsibilities of a leader, as I said in the beginning of this chapter, is to create the vision, forge the path, and lead the team down that path to achieve results. I worked with a large national retailer for many years that did not do this. They had a vision to reinvent their store environment, which is common with retailers these days because they understand that most retail growth is coming from online transactions. Retailers are fighting now for physical store visits because those visits are down, and many retailers fear they are going to continue to decline. Many are recreating their store environments and product mixes and assortments so they can attract more customers.

This particular retailer claimed they were going to totally recreate their store environment, and after a couple of months, had a new store concept ready to show their suppliers. They revealed the store of the future and proclaimed that in one year, they were going to launch this new concept in every single store. This was a retailer with numerous rooftops, and the feedback they received was consistent across the board—no one could see how they were going to be able to roll out this concept to hundreds, if not thousands, of stores within a year. This retailer had already made a commitment, however, and was determined to make it happen.

After a couple of months, they did get a store installed, and after another month of gathering feedback, it was clear that the new concept was not working. Neither the product mix nor the store environment were quite right. They eliminated a good deal of product to create a cleaner store environment, which is very common among retailers, but they had cut away too much of their product mix, and the concept simply didn't work. The retail team was embarrassed. When the project was finally finished and they had failed to meet their goals, they had lost the confidence of the supplier community, and the leaders in charge of the new concept stores had lost credibility within their organization. The final complete rollout never came to fruition.

If that retailer had taken the time to create a vision, and then created a path to get there, instead of making the huge, lofty claim that, "We're going to have every store remodeled in a year," they could have met their goal. They should have set their first steps along a path to the future that people could see, and said, “In our first ninety days, we’re going to test our first prototype.” Then they could have planned to evaluate the results sixty days after the launch of the prototype, making any necessary changes and then rolling out to five stores.

What could have followed at that point might have sounded something like, “After ninety days seeing how those five stores perform, we’re going to make what we feel are the appropriate changes at that point and try that new, revised version in ten stores.” After a couple of years, they might have had a store concept they could have rolled out nationwide, but by being so bold and over-the-top with their vision, and so vague on the details of how they were going to get there, they made profound mistakes that cost them their success.

Leaders must lead. Leaders must make the case for change, but it is crucial that they create a path that shows how that change will be accomplished, each step of the way, each step visible from the last, and that they communicate that ultimate vision and the path leading to it in a way that is credible to the team members who will be called upon to execute that change.

Most importantly, you, the leader, must keep growing. Don’t ever stop growing your skills, learning, expanding your expertise, getting better at what you do. Continue to acquire and develop the practical skills you need to lead, and then learn when it’s appropriate to use each of those skills. This is good news because you don’t have to be born a natural leader or master communicator. The skills required to lead can be learned by any smart, motivated, hardworking person.

The critical difference between those who succeed as leaders and those who do not is that those who succeed stay focused throughout the course of their entire careers, and not only master those skills, but also learn over time when to call upon them. If you're doing the extra work, if you're going the extra mile, if you have it in you to be the very best business person you can possibly be, then you will always be looking for new challenges, new lessons to learn, and you will strive to incorporate those new skills into your professional behaviors. By doing this, you will constantly improve over the course of your career.

For Reflection

Using the ten steps outlined in this chapter as a guide for reflection:

Who do you consider a leader with a vision with whom you would like to spend more time?

Who, specifically, do you need to associate yourself with more? Less?

What are some of the big issues that you need to focus on in your business?

What are you most afraid of in terms of being a leader?

Take a good look at how you spend your time each week. In what areas do you need to spend more time, and in what areas do you need to spend less? Are there things you are not spending any time on that deserve your attention?

Where, right now, is the friction on your team or in your organization?

When in your career did you have the most passion?

Part Three

The Education of Experience

In September of 1980, I attended Hallmark sales training, a rigorous and lengthy consultative selling skills course. The lessons were basic—identify a need, understand the need, ask these certain questions, and so on. They were so rudimentary that at times, I would laugh under my breath because they were making it so strictly academic, sterile, and linear. Even at that entry level, I already had several years of sales training under my belt. I worked through all of college and taken on some tough sales jobs long the way. I learned more from practical, hands-on experience than I could ever learn from any textbook, course, or seminar. Tough lessons and hard knocks shaped me into the leader I am today.

Chapter 23

Learning to Close the Deal

My first experience as a salesman was selling pots and pans door-to-door. It's not a concept that anyone would consider today, but almost forty years ago in rural Arkansas, we sold what we called a "hope chest." The idea was that we put together a package of housewares—pots and pans and other cookware, tableware, and flatware—that a single woman, either working or in college, would buy in the "hope" that she would one day get married and have this set-up of goods to bring into the relationship. It's a ridiculous notion nowadays, and rightfully insulting to many people, but back then, we incorporated the idea of this need into our targeting and sales pitches to our customers, and it was highly successful.

Our two peak sales times of the year were when female nursing students would gather in Little Rock, Arkansas to take their certification exams. The exams were held at the Medical Center, and the university would put the nursing students up in dorm rooms during the testing days. There would be hundreds of single young women visiting Little Rock, and my friends and I would go to the building where the exams were being held and hang out outside.

In the breaks between exams, or when the women wanted to smoke a cigarette (which a lot of people did back in the late seventies), they stepped outside. Two other pot and pan salesmen and I would approach them and say, "We have a free gift for you if you'll let us come by your room tonight and give you a quick presentation."

The gift was a little spoon ring—just a small ring that looked like a spoon. We each bought them by the hundreds for a dollar a-piece. We were young, clean-cut college boys, and the nurses were always housed together in large groups, so they were comfortable with us coming by to give them their gift. We made a lot of appointments for our demonstrations this way. It was the perfect opportunity to get to present to large groups all at the same time. We might bring a six pack of beer and just visit casually with the girls, and we almost always made several sales every single evening during those times of the year. We had the flexibility to put customers on payment plans over several months, whatever they could afford, so that even full-time students would not be intimidated by the cost of our product sets.

I remember one day when a woman told me, "I don't have time to hear your sales pitch. I need to exercise, so I'm going to go swim."

"That's okay," I replied, "I'll go down to the pool with you." I walked with her down to the pool, and she started swimming laps. She swam down to the other end of the pool and then back, lifted her head up out of the water and asked, "Okay, what have you got?"

I think that rejection, along with success, taught me solid selling skills.

I talked a little bit, then she'd swim down and back, and I'd continue my pitch for a few moments before she'd be off and swimming again. The pitch that usually took about an hour was taking me double that to get through, and it got to be sort of a joke after a while because just when I felt like I was about to close, she would stop me and swim off. This girl just kept swimming and swimming, but after almost two hours, while she was still in the pool, I finished my pitch, got her to reach up out of the water, and sign the order page, and I walked out.

I'm not sure how many college kids would take this job and have the discipline to do it every day. Clearly, you had to park your ego at the door because it was not an attractive job to most people. To do that job, which was paid only by commission, you had to allow yourself to be put in some incredibly uncomfortable situations, to take risks, and accept rejection on a constant basis. I think that rejection, along with success, taught me solid selling skills. I learned to listen to everything. Many times, there would be a friend in the home with the client, or the homeowner's mother would be there. As I got more experienced, I learned how much time to spend on each section of the pitch. I had to listen to what everyone was saying and tailor my presentation on the fly.

I would often lean to a mother and say, "I have a set of this cookware and I just love it." Sometimes, a boyfriend or husband would be there and they would talk about how expensive it was. I made sure to mention later in the presentation that it was only twenty dollars a month, less than a lunch out, or other comparisons. There was always an answer to an objection, a rebuttal for every reason they couldn't buy.

My big takeaway from this experience was that I learned to listen and handle objections during my presentation, rather than waiting until the close. If a salesperson knows the major objections to their pitch and can deal with them during the presentation, their closing rate should improve. After I'd gotten enough experience to run a smooth presentation, my closure rate was more than fifty percent. Listen to the objections. Deal with them during the pitch and you will close more often than you otherwise would.

For Reflection

What was your first job? What skills and lessons did you learn? How are those skills and lessons still useful and impactful for you today?

Chapter 24

On the Job Training

I stopped selling pots and pans after a while and started selling Kirby vacuum cleaners because at the time, I thought there was a much bigger market, and it paid better and quicker. Sometimes, it took ninety-plus days to get the commission check for the pots and pans, which seemed like an eternity to a college kid. Plus, selling pots and pans that had a lifetime warranty made me think I would eventually run out of clients to sell to, but I figured that almost everyone who owned a home also needed a vacuum cleaner, and those don't last forever. Selling vacuum cleaners meant simply going door-to-door, which I was already comfortable doing, and it turned out to be incredibly lucrative.

I landed the job by answering an ad in the paper for a small company hiring reps to sell Kirby vacuums. I told the woman who was hiring that I had sold pots and pans, so she figured I could probably sell vacuum cleaners, but first, I had to learn all the technical aspects of the machine and how it worked. This took a couple of weeks. Then, when I thought I was ready, a woman named Margaret went with me on my first sales call. We went to a house occupied by two women, presumably sisters. I gave them my sales pitch, which took about two hours, and these ladies were tough. They asked hard questions and made me thoroughly demonstrate everything about the vacuum. I ended up cleaning most of their house!

At the end of my lengthy demonstration, they signed the order. It was the toughest pitch I ever had to make, but I made my first sale. Margaret said, "Okay, I see you can do it, you're out on your own now."

In hindsight, I think that first supervised sales call was at a home where Margaret took all her new potential salespeople. Once you got to a point where she thought you could sell, she'd let you go, and so if you could sell to her two friends, she'd know you were ready, and she'd even pay you for the sale so it seemed like a real sales call. It was brilliant on her part to make sure you were successful on your first sales call. About a year later, I heard another salesman say, "I just made my first sale to two ladies named Betty and Thelma. I think they were sisters."

Friends of mine were working at burger places or retail, making three or four dollars an hour, but I could make four or five hundred dollars if I had a good weekend.

When I heard that, I thought, "Wait, those are the same ladies who...oh, I get it." Those two ladies must have bought a whole housefull of vacuum cleaners and had the cleanest carpets in town.

Friends of mine were working at burger places or retail, making three or four dollars an hour, but I could make four or five hundred dollars if I had a good weekend. Not every weekend was great, but the experience I gleaned from selling pots and pans helped me close a high percentage of sales. Seventy to eighty percent of the time, when I was invited in to someone's house, I was able to close. I figured out how to get into more homes by using a system of referrals. If I made a sale, before I left, I asked the homeowner if she had any friends who she thought would be interested in a vacuum cleaner. If someone called ahead of time to make an appointment for me, and a woman was expecting me at the door, then I was guaranteed to be invited in. If I got in, I was likely going to close. This method of referrals greatly increased my percentage of quality prospects and successful sales.

I had to make two hundred dollars selling the vacuum cleaner to pay for the unit. Anything over that was mine to keep, so if I had a customer at around the three hundred seventy-five or four-hundred-dollar mark, I'd be willing to give them ten dollars off for every name they gave me as a referral, up to ten names. If she had a sister or sister-in-law or daughter, and would call and tell them I'm a decent guy and they should let me come over and show them this great new vacuum cleaner, I'd take ten dollars off the price right then and there.

It was a great incentive for the customer, and I'd give up as much as one hundred dollars of my commission. Other salespeople thought I was crazy for giving up that money, but I had learned the benefit of a qualified prospect—someone who was expecting me. If someone referred me, I was way more likely to close the deal.

I wouldn't always get ten names, but I often got four or five, and I considered that a success. I was willing to give up that money because I knew that seven out of ten times I walked into the house of a qualified prospect, I was going to make that sale. For each of those customers, I'd give the same ten-dollar discount to get more names, and I'd go from there.

During this time, I worked with a man named Al Peterson. Back then, he was what we called a "Bo Jacker," which meant he sold everything. That's how he got in the door selling vacuum cleaners. He was the one who taught me the art of observation. When you walk into someone's home, try to capture as quickly as you can everything that goes on in there. How many people live there? Do they have kids? Do they have hobbies? Do they sew? Do they hunt? Do they play golf or tennis? You could see all these items lying around the house, and all these things were now in negotiation for the vacuum cleaner. Everything was in play. This guy was a selling artist. Within a minute or two upon entering a home, he had a clear picture in his mind about what that family's life was like. He was amazing.

> *What I learned from him was that I was not just selling vacuum cleaners. I was trying to get the prospect whatever it was they wanted.*

He even had his own little warehouse where he kept all the items he bartered during a sales call. He had golf clubs, guns, coolers, refrigerators, sewing machines, you name it. Sewing machines were a big item around there back then. Al was making more money by far on the resale of the other items he took in than he ever made selling vacuum cleaners.

What I learned from him was that I was not just selling vacuum cleaners. I was trying to get the prospect whatever it was they wanted. They might need a refrigerator, or bike, or TV, or stereo. He had crafted the skills of observation and listening to such a high degree, he rarely left any presentation without selling, trading, or buying something. He did this three to four times a day, every day. A lot of people are great sales people, but this guy was the best I've ever seen.

I took what he taught me very seriously and tried to put it to work whenever I could. There were many times when I'd go into a home and see that the family didn't have much money. Maybe they even lived in a mobile home or a small apartment. These vacuums were a pricy item, starting at over four hundred dollars, and this was northwest Arkansas in the mid-seventies. There were few high-income neighborhoods, but one of the first lessons you learn as a salesman is not to assume anything about whether your customer has money. They might have plenty of money and are just living this way for any number of reasons.

When it came time to talk price, I'd start with the truth, "It's $429.95."

The customer might say, "I can't afford that. I just bought this Sears Kenmore vacuum for eighty dollars. Your vacuum is better, but it's just too expensive."

I would continue, "I'll give you eighty dollars for that Kenmore, right here, right now, so $429.95 minus $80 makes it $349.95."

If the husband was there and I noticed he was a hunter, I'd say, "I see you're a hunter. Do you have any old guns you don't use?"

He might say, "Sure, I've got this old shotgun, but I just bought this new one," and we'd start talking about hunting and the new gun.

Then I'd say, "I'll tell you what. I'll give you a hundred dollars for the shotgun and take another hundred dollars off the price of the vacuum."

That would knock the price down to just under two hundred, fifty dollars, and that would start to sound more affordable to the customer. I'd have to go through all these theatrics about calling my boss to get special permission to commit to this sort of special deal that nobody else was ever going to get. Back then we didn't have cell phones, so I'd have to ask the customer if I could use the phone in the house to call my boss and make sure this special deal was okay. I would tell the customer, "If I do this, if I call my boss and explain to her what I'm trying to do here, I'm not going to be able to go back on it. Are you okay with that?"

If they agreed, they would show me to the phone, and I'd call Margaret. She'd answer, "Alright, say what you gotta say," and I'd go into my act about how these are really nice folks who could really benefit from the vacuum, I think it would make a much-needed positive change in their lives. I'd go on, "Now, don't laugh at me, but they've got this old Kenmore vacuum that I've agreed to give them eighty dollars for, and they've got this old shotgun that I've agreed to give them a hundred dollars for, but I think we can do something with those items. Are you okay with that?" Then I'd pretend to be listening to her go on and on about this great deal she was straining to agree to.

Finally, I'd say "Okay, okay. I'll be back in the office in a few hours. We can talk about it then. I can make it right, I promise." I'd hang up the phone and declare, "Okay, we've got a deal."

Margaret was never saying anything on the other end of the line. She just had the phone tucked under her chin while she did paperwork with a cigarette in her mouth, waiting for me to hang up.

I would take that other vacuum and the shotgun and leave them in my car, and before too long, you can bet I would end up at a small house or mobile home or apartment where it was immediately clear that these folks could not afford the four hundred-plus dollar vacuum cleaner. Maybe I'd find out they didn't even own a vacuum cleaner, so I'd say, "Hey, I've got this old Kenmore vacuum in my truck, I'll sell it to you for fifty dollars."

They'd get a good deal and be able to own a vacuum cleaner. I already made my margin on the deal that got me the Kenmore, and the fifty dollars was maybe my gas money for the week or something. That sort of dealing went on all the time.

I also learned from Al how to ask just the right questions to strengthen my sales pitch. Once I got in the door and began my demonstration, I'd ask, "Do you have a room that needs shampooing?" Of course, they did. Everybody does. It would take about thirty minutes to shampoo the carpet. Then, I would continue my presentation, and after fifteen minutes or so, if the homeowner wanted me to leave, I'd go, but as I was shampooing and presenting, I would start a conversation. "Do you have kids?"

I already knew the answer because I'd seen children's toys or photos around the house already. I'd ask, "Do your kids ever suffer from allergies? Do they ever get sick?"

Of course, I knew they got sick because every kid gets sick, so I'd ask to see the child's bedroom. I'd go to the bed, pull back the sheets, take the bag out of the vacuum and place a small black cloth over the bag end of the hose. I'd run the vacuum and pull it two or three times across the bed, and every time, without fail, the black cloth would go flying off the other end because it had become caked with dirt and hair and debris of all kinds. This is the point where I would make my sale. I'd show the wife the dirt from the bed and she would turn to her husband and say, "I told you we needed a new vacuum cleaner!"

The husband was the same guy who, when I first walked into the house, said, "We're not buying a vacuum cleaner today. I don't know what you're even doing here because the last thing we're going to do is buy a vacuum cleaner." Usually, he turned out to be right. The last thing he did before I left was buy a vacuum cleaner.

Eventually, I had to move on from the vacuum cleaner business because I decided to go to graduate school, and it was just too time-consuming. There were moments I considered taking a couple of years off to sell full time like Al. He made more than a hundred thousand dollars a year doing what he did, and I thought that if I made half of that, I'd be making far more than any corporate job would pay me after graduate school.

I talked to my dad about it. He said, "Sure, you can make fifty thousand dollars a year, but do you want to be selling vacuum cleaners door-to-door when you're fifty years old?" Again, the man steered me in the right direction.

I still had to have some sort of job to pay rent and buy food, so during graduate school, I worked at one of the first automatic drive-through car washes. My job there was to sell different car wash options to customers who pulled in to fill up with gas. I got paid a three-dollar-per-hour base to help people pump gas, and I'd just talk to them as I was helping them. I'd talk about the car, the weather, the road conditions, and as these folks saw all those other cars being washed and brightened up, turning the conversation toward the sales pitch was easy.

I sold a polish wash, a polish wax, a tire bright, and an air freshener. I earned two dollars if I sold a wax, another two if I sold a tire bright, and a dollar if I sold an air freshener. This was another great sales experience. I had to walk up to people all day long and convince them to buy from me. I worked to get something out of every car, even if it was just the air freshener, but if I sold a wax, a tire bright, and an air freshener all together, I'd make five dollars from that one car. On a typical Saturday, we'd wash a hundred and fifty cars, so I could make some serious money.

One day, a man I'd seen before pulled up. I gave him the usual talk, "Hey, buddy! My boss wants to make sure all our best customers leave with their cars looking great today. I see you've been smoking in the car, so maybe it's time to put some new pine scent in there."

He asked me, "What do you do?" I told him I was in graduate school studying business. He worked for an insurance company, and as he handed me his business card, he told me to call and set up a time to come see him. I did, and he offered me a job on the spot. He said, "As soon as you graduate, come work for me. Sell insurance right here. In fact, you can start right now, while you're still a student."

While I appreciated his offer, I turned him down because selling insurance didn't seem like something I would enjoy. I would have preferred to go back to selling vacuum cleaners and bartering with homeowners, which was sometimes fun. It was encouraging, however, to have a total stranger recognize my skills and offer to hire me like that right on the spot.

I am thankful my dad steered me in the right direction, encouraging me to stay in school and earn my master's degree, and I am equally thankful that I didn't end up selling insurance. The career I have had at Hallmark for over three decades has been an amazing gift, but when I went to the sales training back in 1980 and they were trying to teach me how to "identify the need," I knew I was way beyond all that. I had learned from experience how to do it. I'd received my sales education by getting out there and doing the job, and that was the best training I could have ever received.

For Reflection

What were some of your early successes that shaped you in business? What were some of your early failures? Of all your early experiences, which has the greatest impact on you today and why?

Chapter 25

Under the Gun

After I sold vacuum cleaners but before I began selling car washes, I had another job for a brief time—I repossessed cars. Talk about "on the job training!" The father of one of my college friends owned a repossession company out of Little Rock, and he needed people in Fayetteville, where we went to school, to collect cars and other items from people who had defaulted on their loans. To say this was a rough job would be an understatement.

We made badges that read, "Arkansas Recovery Agent," had our pictures taken to make them look official, and put the badges and photos in badge wallets we purchased. Now, we had no real authority whatsoever. All these badges did was make us feel like we did. We were just two, twenty-two-year-old kids with these meaningless badges, who showed up and announced with all the command we could muster, "Arkansas Recovery Agents! We're here to pick up your vehicle, sir!"

To say the least, the skills I learned while doing this job were very different than the skills I learned selling vacuum cleaners. First and foremost, I had to summon the courage to just show up to do this job because it was pretty scary sometimes. I also had to learn to drive eighteen-wheelers, motorcycles, tractors, busses. It took a lot of muscle, too.

We had to carry out TVs, refrigerators, bed sets, you name it, and I did this dozens of times.

We had to collect every manner of vehicle or item, no matter how strange. On one job, we got a call from our boss in Little Rock describing what we were going to be looking for—a minibus that someone had converted into an RV. The owner had not made a payment in many months, and he was suspected to be "somewhere in northwestern Arkansas, near the town of Mountain Home." When we received information on a repossession, we were rarely given a specific address. Usually, it was a rural route number of some sort.

We drove for two hours to Mountain Home, Arkansas and stopped at the post office to ask where "Rural Route Whatever" was. We then drove out on this old dirt road, and sure enough, we finally came across the minibus turned RV.

When we pulled up, we were met by an older gentleman, probably seventy years old, and his granddaughter. As we walked toward him, he asked, "You here for the bus?"

We nodded, "Yep."

"Just sit down a second," he said. "You want a beer or something?"

We sat down under a shade tree, and he started telling us this sad story about his wife dying, and then he ran through a list of all the things he'd lost in his life. He added, "But the good news is that I've been working really hard, I've gotten some good jobs lately, and a guy is coming up here tomorrow to pay me for the work. So tomorrow, I'll have the money to get caught up on my payments on the bus. If you could just come back here first thing tomorrow morning, I'll have your money for you. You can even stay here if you want. I've got nowhere to put you, so you'll have to sleep in your truck, or if you go back into town, find a decent hotel, come back here in the morning, I'll have your money for you."

He was an old guy with his little granddaughter sitting right there, and his wife was gone, so we thought that it seemed fair. To be honest, we just felt bad for him. We pulled away, found our way back to a pay phone, called our boss and gave him the story that he'd get his money tomorrow. Our boss exploded, "What?! I don't care what that S.O.B. said! You go back and you get that bus NOW! He'll be gone tomorrow!"

I learned a very important lesson early on in this job. People will look you in the eye, with incredible sincerity, and even sometimes tears, and lie straight to your face. Some people are professional liars.

We knew he meant business, so we drove right back there and explained to the guy that our boss told us to take the bus. "But if you take the bus and then I get the money tomorrow, I'll have to start over anyway," he pleaded. "If you just come back tomorrow, you'll be saving an old man from having to start over with his granddaughter to look after."

He was as sincere and genuine as you can imagine. We thought this old guy deserved a break, so we drove back to town without the bus and found a motel for a few bucks. After a cheap dinner and a horrible night's sleep, we headed back up the road first thing in the morning.

When we arrived, guess what we found? Minibus, old man, and granddaughter—long gone. I realize that every reader could've seen that coming a mile away, but we were young, what can I say? We got our butts chewed out because of that, and probably would have lost our jobs, but because my partner's dad was our boss, we were safe.

I learned a very important lesson early on in this job. People will look you in the eye, with incredible sincerity, and even sometimes tears, and lie straight to your face. Some people are professional liars.

I learned another important lesson on this job on my twenty-second birthday, January 18, 1978. We received a call to repossess a pickup truck in Farmington, Arkansas. Again, the address we were given was "somewhere along a rural route," and as our boss was giving us the details over the phone, he said, "The place is a little bit of a cult."

"What exactly do you mean, a *little bit* of a cult?" I asked.

He said, "I'm just reading you the paper the bank gave me. I'm sure it's nothing." He always deflected and downsized any sort of bad news, so we should've been a little leery, but again, we were young and needed the money, so we drove out to that rural route late in the cold, snowy, January evening. We found the house sitting back, about a hundred and fifty feet from the road, with the front gate locked. We couldn't see the truck and didn't even know for sure if it was there.

We parked up the road and waited until about midnight when we thought it safe to take a closer look. We hopped the fence, walked all the way up to the house, and found the truck. The keys weren't in it, but for this particular job, we had a key. That wasn't always the case. If we didn't get a key for a repossession, back then, you could use a lock pull or a slide hammer, depending on the make of the vehicle. You exposed the lock however you knew how, and could use a screwdriver to turn the ignition. We were always prepared with these tools just in case, but because we had a key for this job, it should've been easy.

We knew we'd be able to start the truck, but that didn't help us with the locked front gate. We figured we could try to break the lock when we got there, but we discovered another problem first. The truck was full of firewood. We didn't see any lights on in the house, so we didn't know if they had electricity. We assumed they were probably living through the winter by the heat of a wood burning stove. Although we knew we needed to get out of there quickly, I said to my friend, "Before we go, let's just throw the firewood out. They must really need it."

My friend agreed, and he climbed up in the truck bed and started throwing the wood out onto the ground while I shoved the pile away from the truck. We were almost ready to get out of there when I heard the distinctive sound of a cocked shotgun, immediately followed by the unmistakable feeling of the gun barrel pressed against my back. I froze.

"What the #%&@ are you doin'?" a rough, gravelly voice demanded from behind.

"Arkansas Recovery Agents!" We fumbled for our make-shift badges. "We're here representing Bank of America. We've come up from Little Rock to recover your vehicle due to lack of payment."

Still holding the gun to my back, the man growled, "We don't believe you. We think you're just here stealing our stuff. We could just shoot you, kill you right here, right now, bury you out in the pasture, and nobody would ever know you were even here."

"Please don't do that! We're here on official business! We can prove it if you can take us to a phone!"

Without saying a word, they walked us toward a shed out back, which we took as a very bad sign. The property didn't have electricity, but it turned out that they *did* have a phone line running to this shed, and much to our surprise, they were going to let us make the call. At about one o'clock in the morning, we called our boss back in Little Rock. He got on the phone and verified us. "These two young men work for me, and they're gonna get that truck."

The guy with the gun said, "We're not giving them the truck."

Our boss did not back down, "If you don't give my guys the truck, then I'm gonna drive up there tomorrow, and get it myself."

Pointing the gun straight at us, our captor said to our boss, "We'll shoot these two sons of bitches right now... and bury them in the yard."

"You go ahead and shoot 'em if you want to. I'm still comin' to get that truck."

I was thinking, "This is it. This is how it ends. I'm going to die right here, right now, and be dumped in the woods on my twenty-second birthday."

The lesson here is this: try to understand what you're getting yourself into before you get into it.

The guy hung up the phone, and he and his friends proceeded to roughed us up a little bit. They shoved us around, punched us in the stomachs, and threw us off the property into the snow. We ran back to our car and got the heck out of there.

We drove back home, but were so jacked up we couldn't sleep. Once we got over the initial shock of the experience, we were mad—really mad—so about four in the morning we drove back up that dirt road to where we had originally parked. We figured they were going to have to leave the property with that truck at some point, so we waited. A little later that morning, sure enough, the truck pulled off the property. We followed them at a distance down that backcountry road until they parked at a grocery store. When they went inside, we snuck over and took the truck and hightailed it out of there.

We drove it back to Fayetteville, where we had a storage yard. We celebrated getting that truck, and even though no one believed our story, we felt pretty good about it.

After that truck sat in the storage lot for about two months, those guys showed up with proof that they had finally paid it off and were eligible to retake ownership. My friend and I happened to be there when they arrived, and they sure were bent out of shape.

Boy, were they mad at us, but we got the job done, and the bank got their money.

The lesson here is this: try to understand what you're getting yourself into before you get into it. Just because your boss tells you to do something doesn't mean it's a good idea. Sometimes, you must decide on your own course of action. There are times when your boss simply doesn't know all the facts. If we had waited for the truck to be driven off the property instead of rushing in to retrieve it from that very strange place because our boss had told us to, we could have avoided that confrontation altogether.

On another occasion, we got a call to pick up a car in a trailer park in Joplin, Missouri. We arrived at night, found the address, saw the car sitting there, and this time, also had the key. From where we parked, we could see through the windows of the trailer that the owner was still awake watching Johnny Carson. We sat there waiting for him to go to sleep. After quite a while, we saw him turn off the TV and lights and walk to the back of the trailer. We waited maybe another twenty minutes before I walked up, got in, and started the car. Whenever I repossessed a car, I always looked around to see if there was anything in there that the person might need, like a coat or something, and because I thought this repossession was a low-stress assignment, I took an extra moment to look around the car. There was nothing there, so I pulled out, and my friend pulled up behind me.

In the time it took us to line up for our exit, after I had taken the extra minute to check out the car, the guy in the trailer woke up, came running out, got into another car, and began to pursue us. This wasn't the first time this had happened, and we had a plan in place. If we were pursued, the car in back would lag a bit and act as a block, so that the collected car could gain some distance on the angry guy chasing us. We would work out ahead of time where we would meet if we had to separate to get away from somebody.

About an hour later, we met at our predetermined parking lot. We had the car and we had evaded the owner, so we headed back to Arkansas. The next morning, we called our boss to let him know we had collected the car, and he told us that we had to immediately drive that car somewhere, park it, leave it there, and take off.

"Why?"

"Because the guy had that car paid off in full, and you should not have taken it."

"What do you mean?! You had the papers on that car showing he was delinquent!"

It turned out that the paperwork was valid when he received it, but the guy had paid off the car before we got to it, so legally, we were on the wrong side of this one. Basically, we had just committed grand theft auto.

"So, here's what I want you to do," our boss said. "I want you to take that car back to that parking lot, leave the keys in it, wipe it all down, get out of there, and do not talk about this to anyone ever again. I just found out the police are looking for that car."

> The lesson? Be careful. Know the business you're getting involved in, and be aware of what you're doing it for.

I guess my first reaction should have been shock and dismay at the thought that we had essentially stolen this man's car, but it wasn't. My first question was, "Do we still get paid?" We did. We split thirty-five dollars, so we each made $17.50 for taking that poor man's car. I like to think it was found and he got it back, though. Hopefully, that's the case.

The lesson? Be careful. Know the business you're getting involved in, and be aware of what you're doing it for.

Another lesson I learned during this time is how important it is to work for a person or a company that has integrity. On another one of our repo adventures, we got a call to collect a motorcycle, a car, and a TV all from the same person. We had to take a couple of friends with us because we couldn't carry all that stuff by ourselves at once. When we arrived at the house, we knocked on the door, "Arkansas Recovery Agents!"

The man came to the door, relaxed and friendly. "Ya'll just come on in," he said.

"We're here to pick up the motorcycle, the car, and the TV."

He shook his head, "Yeah. We haven't been payin' for 'em. You can have 'em. I'm sorry."

He invited us to sit down, fed us dinner, and helped us load the TV into the car. He even topped off the motorcycle with gas because he knew we had some distance to travel. The bunch of us drove off, one on the motorcycle, one in the car, and two of us in our car with the TV, and I remember looking in my rear-view mirror as we were pulling away. That guy was standing on his porch with his family, and we had just left him with nothing.

Some people *will* lie to you, some *will* chase you. Some will even shoot at you, but it was the folks who were nice and just down on their luck – those were the jobs that made me feel the worst. In fact, that ended up being my last repossession job. I was starting graduate school and needed to devote more time to my studies. After seeing that image in the rear-view mirror that day, I was ready to move on from that job anyway.

It was at that point that I took the job selling car washes. The money I made there was pretty good for a college student, and I decided that it's always better to work at a job where fewer people would like to shoot you.

For Reflection

There's always lessons to be learned, even in difficult situations. What are some valuable lessons you've learned from difficult or even dangerous situations?

Chapter 26

Enjoy the Journey and Don't Take Yourself Too Seriously

As my years of corporate life in a big company draw rapidly to a close, I don't think I'll be telling my grandkids or my friends about all the important meetings I attended, the presentations I delivered, or the product launches that succeeded. I think I'll be talking about all the great people I met, the great relationships I developed, and the humorous experiences I had along the way.

As you travel through your career, I strongly encourage you to take time to enjoy the people you work with. You will meet some wonderful people who have big lives outside of work, and you're going to be fascinated by them and have great times with them. If you spend time building and fostering these relationships, you're going to have some memorable experiences.

I remember back in 1985 when I was a mid-level manager in Dallas, responsible for opening new stores and moving existing stores to better locations. That summer, I was responsible for most of the Dallas/Fort Worth area and almost all of Oklahoma. I was working with a regional sales person in Oklahoma City with a couple of retailers who owned a dozen stores. The two retailers happened to be brothers-in-law, and one of their stores was in the mall in Norman, Oklahoma. Because it was in a small location, we wanted to move it across the hall to a bigger retail space. The brothers-in-law were both pharmacists who ran their retail businesses on the side; they were talented businessmen, very good at negotiation, and we had been negotiating the cost of the move and the floor plan of the larger location with them for many weeks.

I caught an early flight from Dallas to Oklahoma City to finalize the deal so we could start work in time to have the store back up and running before the holiday shopping season that year. The regional sales person picked me up at the airport, and we drove to Paul's Valley, Oklahoma, about an hour south of Oklahoma City, where one of the brothers, Jack, had his pharmacy. We were meeting him there to get his final approval on the store floor plan.

When we arrived, Jack told us that one of his pharmacists was out sick that day so he had to fill a few prescriptions before he could leave. This was one of those old-style pharmacies that carried a little bit of everything and included a small restaurant, so Jack told us to go over and have some lunch and he'd be with us as soon as he could get away.

Over the next hour, the sales rep and I ate lunch and went over the details of the deal. We reviewed the blueprint of the new store layout—where all the aisles were going to be and where the product groups were going to be placed—and we determined cost estimates for the move. Finished with everything we could do without Jack, we checked back at the pharmacy, but he said, "I'm still busy. I called another pharmacist but he's not here yet."

We returned to the restaurant to wait some more, and when we checked in again a little later, Jack was still busy. This went on for hours. We left the pharmacy and walked up and down the main street of the little town, taking turns making phone calls at the only payphone booth we could find.

Finally, around four o'clock, Jack said he needed to run an errand and invited us to join him. Thinking we could talk business on the way, we climbed in his three-quarter ton workingman's pickup, threw our briefcases and travel bags in the back, and headed about thirty minutes out to his farm. When we got there, he pulled around to where he kept the livestock and said, "I have to vaccinate some cattle."

Slightly perplexed at why this needed to happen right now, we said, "Sure, okay. We'll hang back and..."

"No, no, no," he interjected. "This is not a one-man job. I asked you to come along because I need you guys to help me."

He positioned the sales rep out in the fenced-in pen where the cattle were kept. His job was to drive the cattle toward the chute, where I would hold them still so Jack could vaccinate them. I'd shove them out into another pen, and then we'd get the next cow into the chute.

Over the course of the next three hours, we vaccinated sixty-seven head of cattle in the sweltering Oklahoma summertime heat. By the end of it all, we were sweating right through our suits. We had our coats off and our ties loose, we were filthy, and from the knees down we were caked with mud and manure. When we finally finished, Jack said, "I've worked up an appetite. Let's go get something to eat."

By this point, the sales rep and I were looking at each other thinking, "What are we doing?" Jack was an important customer. He owned a dozen stores, so our relationship with him was critical, especially in the middle of a rather large and time sensitive negotiation, so we continued to accommodate his requests. We were both thinking that dinner would finally be the time to have the conversation we needed to have with him.

We drove fifteen minutes to his favorite barbeque place only to find a bunch of his friends there drinking. Jack ordered a couple of pitchers of beer and settled in. Finally, I spoke up, "Hey, Jack, we really do need to take a look at this..."

He cut me off, "Let's eat first."

"Look," I continued, trying not to reveal my frustration and exhaustion, "I've got a flight back tomorrow morning and I'd like to get this done..."

"Hey, hey, hey," he interrupted. "First things first."

Complying, we ate dinner, drank our beer, and talked to his friends. As soon as I felt I could bring it up again, I said, "Jack, could we *please*, please look at this floor plan?"

"Oh, the floor plan?" he grinned. "Me and Jay decided on that yesterday. We're good to go. We're all set with that," and then he just laughed and laughed.

As you are going through your career, traveling around, meeting people, experiencing all the different situations and obstacles in your assignments, take the time to enjoy the lighter side of the complications you run into along the way.

It turned out I didn't need to fly to Oklahoma. I didn't need to drive to Paul's Valley. I didn't need to hang out in a drug store and stand by a pay phone on Main Street all afternoon, and I certainly didn't need to vaccinate sixty-seven head of cattle in my suit and tie.

To this day, when I see Jack, or get a message from him, he always asks me if I'm available to go vaccinate some cattle. That's the kind of experience that creates a relationship that lasts a long time.

I remember another funny episode with my good friend Jim who rose through the company ranks with me. One year, I was assigned to a task force that was doing some strategy work, and we were sent to attend a large sales meeting in Las Vegas. We flew out early in the morning, hoping we would arrive in time to have lunch at the meeting. We got to the hotel at noon, Vegas time, which was really two o'clock our time, so we were famished and thrilled that we were in time for lunch. We were escorted to our table, which was one of those large, round, ten-person tables. Jim was sitting a couple of tables away from me, but in my line of vision.

Lunch was scheduled after the next session, but it started to run long. By one o'clock Vegas time (three o'clock Kansas City time), we were beyond starving. On each of the tables were these enormous, beautiful centerpieces, ornately arranged with flowers and ribbons. Stuffed in each were dozens of full sized chocolate candy bars. I think the theme of this session was "Get in Your Sweet Spot" or something like that which made these huge candy bar centerpieces make sense.

I looked over at Jim and noticed him subtly sneak a candy bar off the centerpiece and eat it. A few minutes later, I looked over again and he was eating another one. A few minutes later, I looked over and he was eating a third candy bar and dropping the wrappers under his chair. In no time, I counted at least five or six candy bar wrappers strewn underneath him on the floor. He was eating his way through this entire gigantic centerpiece, so much so, that it was starting to look lopsided.

I was trying to conceal my laughter, trying to act as if I didn't notice. Finally, the session drew to a close, and the audience was asked to participate. The woman leading announced, "I have a surprise for everyone. If each of you would look under your seat, someone at each table has a red star stuck to the underside of their chair."

Someone at every table found a star underneath their seat. That person took off the star and held it up in the air, awaiting their instructions.

The woman continued, "Everyone holding a red star just won the centerpiece at your table!"

When the woman who had won the centerpiece at Jim's table saw that he had destroyed his side of it by consuming ten or twelve candy bars, she was so shocked and disappointed that she started to cry. She yelled out, "Jim ate my centerpiece! Jim ate my centerpiece!"

Poor Jim was absolutely mortified. He jumped up from his chair, ran out of the ballroom, and returned a few minutes later carrying an armful of mints and gum and hard candy he had purchased at the hotel gift chop. He sat back down at his table, and with everyone watching, desperately tried to stick all these small boxes of mints and packs of gum into the centerpiece. His efforts only made this ornate arrangement look that much worse and did little to assuage the woman whose prize he had devoured.

Jim has since moved on from the company as a very successful consultant and professional speaker. He is a high-level executive who commands a great deal of respect in his field. I see Jim occasionally and deal with him professionally, and on the few occasions when he gets serious and becomes adamant about making a point based on his expertise in a certain area, I always say, "Hey Jim, just don't eat my centerpiece." That's always a guaranteed tension breaker with him. We laugh and then we're ready to dig back in.

I've gathered so many stories like these over all my years in business. As you are going through your career, traveling around, meeting people, experiencing all the different situations and obstacles in your assignments, take the time to enjoy the lighter side of the complications you run into along the way. I barely remember what that seminar topic was, but I'll never forget my friend Jim trying to stuff those little boxes of mints into that centerpiece. Enjoy the people. It's those people and those experiences you will remember the most fondly. Don't forget to have fun.

For Reflection

Take the time to remember the funny moments and experiences you've had along the way. Who are some of the people who've made you laugh? What is one anecdote you could share with others about a humorous experience in business? Do you use humor to cut the tension or defuse difficult situations?

Chapter 27

At the End of the Day

By the time I graduated, I had accumulated such a wide array of experiences—selling pots and pans, vacuum cleaners, and the whole car repossession gig. What I have come to realize is that all the experiences you acquire, especially when you're younger, really add up to an invaluable arsenal of skills. The majority of my buddies were spending their time doing things far more typical for guys in their early twenties—hanging out at the pool hall at night, drinking beer, and meeting girls—all things I would have rather been doing. The fact that I had no money if I didn't work meant I had to always work. Because I wanted to get that education, I was willing to risk walking into somebody's house to try to sell them a set of pots and pans, spend a half-hour shampooing their carpet in the hope of selling them a vacuum cleaner, and make $17.50 to take some poor guy's car. I learned skills.

When I got to Hallmark sales training, I thought it relatively easy compared to what I had been doing. As they were teaching me about selling to a retailer who needed everything we sold and who bought from very few other companies, I remember thinking to myself, "This isn't even sales. This is just showing up."

The work I did when I was young, however modest it may have been, however reckless it may have sometimes been, prepared me and taught me invaluable life lessons. It helped me to build a foundation that allowed me to join a great company like Hallmark and hit the ground running.

Also, because I went to the University of Arkansas, I took great pride in the fact that I could work shoulder to shoulder with people who had attended Harvard, Notre Dame, Stanford, and Indiana. I admire those schools and those people, but I didn't have those same opportunities, and that's okay. The work I did while I was in school had real, practical, and immediate application after I graduated. I think there was something inside me that drove me to take all those risks, to do some not-so-typical jobs. Nobody else did all the things I did, or earned that experience in the same way that I had.

That wide and unique range of experiences gave me the set of skills that laid the foundation for what I do now. For people who are just coming up in the work force or are looking to do something different with their careers, the best way to do it is to just go do it. Learn by experience. And you only do that if you pursue those experiences. I heard someone say once, "Chase skills, don't chase job titles."

My leadership philosophy is relevant when considering this. A leadership philosophy can only be built on a foundation of experience. That makes someone's leadership philosophy a very personal thing. It's based on the combination of experiences that only you have had. My philosophy is based on how I view things and it is uniquely mine. I'll never believe or advocate that because it is mine, it should also be yours. Yours will be based on the unique combination of experiences you have had up to the point when you start to articulate your leadership philosophy. That is also why it can and should change over time. It should develop as you develop, improve as you improve, and it will become more effective as you become more effective.

Whatever success I have had in my thirty-eight years at Hallmark Cards is largely because I sold vacuum cleaners and pots and pans and chased down those guys to repossess their cars. That wide and unique range of experiences gave me the set of skills that laid the foundation for what I do now. For people who are just coming up in the work force or are looking to do something different with their careers, the best way to do it is to just go do it. Learn by experience. And you only do that if you pursue those experiences. I heard someone say once, "Chase skills, don't chase job titles."

Develop skills. You can only do that through experiences, and to put yourself in a place where you are able to tackle those experiences, you've got to take some risks and face some challenges. You've got to put yourself out there. Work hard, stay focused, and never stop learning. If you do this, you're giving yourself the best chance of success in whatever it is you choose to do.

If you want to get better at something, don't let yourself be sidetracked by taking a job because it has an impressive title. Job titles don't mean anything—vice president, senior vice president, CEO—don't pay any attention to that. What do you do? What are you good at? That's what really counts.

Develop skills. You can only do that through experiences, and to put yourself in a place where you are able to tackle those experiences, you've got to take some risks and face some challenges. You've got to put yourself out there. Work hard, stay focused, and never stop learning. If you do this, you're giving yourself the best chance of success in whatever it is you choose to do.

If you are as fortunate in your career as I have been, then you will reach a point one day when you feel the accumulation of your accomplishments. You will have created an ever-growing list of successes and you will understand and have learned from your mistakes. You will feel respected by the people you most respect, and most satisfying of all, you will see the long line of people who you feel you may have had some hand in helping along the way.

I wish you every success in the world.

For Reflection

What in this book has resonated with you? Determine at least three action steps you can take immediately because of something that resonated with you—write them down and then, do them!

Suggestions for Further Reading

Adler, M. J. *How to Speak How to Listen*. (1983). New York, NY: Touchstone.

Album, M. *The Five People You Meet in Heaven*. (2003). New York, NY: Hyperion.

Citrin, J. & Smith, R. *The 5 Patterns of Extraordinary Careers: The Guide for Achieving Success and Satisfaction*. (2005). New York, NY: Crown.

Downs, Alan *The Fearless Executive: Finding the Courage to Trust Your Talents and Be the Leader You Were Meant to Be*. (2000). New York, NY: AMACOM.

Heifetz, R. A., & Linsky, M. *Leadership on the Line: Staying Alive through the Dangers of Leading*. (2002). Boston, MA: Harvard Business School Press.

Johnson, S. *The Present: The gift that Makes you Happier and More Successful at Work and in Life, Today!* (2003). New York, NY: Doubleday.

Lencioni, P. *The Five Dysfunctions of a Team: A Leadership Fable*. (2002). San Francisco, CA: Jossey-Bass.

Maxwell, J. *The 21 Indispensable Qualities of a Leader: Becoming the Person Others Will Want to Follow*. (1999). Nashville, TN: Thomas Nelson.

McCall Jr., M. *Lessons of Experience: How Successful Executives Develop on the Job*. (1988). New York, NY: Free Press.

Myersbriggs.org. (2015). *The Myers & Briggs Foundation - The 16 MBTI® Types*. [online] Available at: http://www.myersbriggs.org/my-mbti-personality-type/mbti-basics/the-16-mbti-types.htm.

Patterson, K., Grenny, J., McMillan, R., & Switzler, A. *Crucial Conversations: Tools for Talking When Stakes Are High*. (2002). New York, NY: McGraw-Hill.

Slywotzky, A. & Morrison, D. *The Profit Zone: How Strategic Business Design Will Lead You to Tomorrow's Profits*. (1997). New York, NY: Three Rivers Press.

Zook, C. & Allen, J. *Profit from The Core: A Return to Growth in Turbulent Times*. (2001). Brighton Watertown, MA: Harvard Business.

About the Authors

Wayne Strickland lives in Kansas City with his wife, Aviva, and is father of four and grandfather to three. He genuinely wishes to share the many lessons he's learned from his accomplished career working with some of the world's largest retailers. As that career draws to a close, Wayne is anxiously looking forward to the next chapter, which he hopes will include lots of time with family and travel around the world. In addition to writing books, his next big project will involve speaking engagements and seminars. He feels a tremendous sense of responsibility to help those coming up the ladder in the business world just as others helped him along the way. Wayne is passionate about people development and leadership accomplished through principle and integrity. He believes leaders who fail do so because they lack competitive intelligence. Find out more about Wayne and how he can help you and your business at www.WayneStricklandSpeaking.com.

Tina Wendling is a freelance writer who is passionate about helping others tell their stories. She works primarily as a ghostwriter and editor to make her client's dreams of writing and publishing a book become reality. Whether it's a personal memoir, business book, web copy, workshop manual, or children's book, she offers a keen eye for detail and insight into her clients' varied perspectives, allowing her to capture the precise style, voice, and messaging her clients are trying to convey. Tina lives in Kansas City with her husband and two sons. Find out more about Tina's writing and editing services at www.eggheadwriting.com.

22672503R00134

Made in the USA
Lexington, KY
14 December 2018